"I've spent the last 15 years pursuing my own character development and teaching others to do the same. Every day we are faced with decisions. Each decision made either enhances or damages our character. It has been said, 'Character takes a lifetime to build, but a split second to lose.' This book isn't just about sports lessons—it's about life lessons. Adults and children will benefit—adults by internalizing and applying, children by receiving and using. I'm excited to see how this book will be used to help people develop true biblical character allowing them to be strong to the finish!"

—*Rod Handley, Founder and President of Character*
That Counts; former Senior Vice President and
COO/CFO of Fellowship of Christian Athletes

"When analyzing performance and success in sports and in life, this book offers a range of exact needs. The thought process instilled by this reading is unique, directing, and very healthy for the mind and body."

—*Dan Gable, 1972 Freestyle Wrestling Olympic Gold*
Medalist; Head Wrestling Coach, University of Iowa
1978-1998

"There is a great need for balance in amateur sports today. The thirst for winning, stardom, and money by players, coaches and parents has resulted in a 'win at any cost' and 'it is all about me' attitude. Teaching and modeling character is being pushed to the background. In the Bible, Jesus, who coached His disciples to change the world, provides us the living example of a coach and the wisdom of how to coach. In this book you will find truths from the Word of God presented—and their application to coaching—that will positively impact the lives of players, coaches and parents."

—*Jim Haney, Executive Director, National Association*
of Basketball Coaches

COACHING
FOR
Character

Dr. Dan Gerdes

Evergreen
PRESS

ISBN 1-58169-126-2
For Worldwide Distribution
Printed in the U.S.A.

Evergreen Press
P.O. Box 191540 • Mobile, AL 36619
800-367-8203

Table of Contents

INTRODUCTION

Athletic experiences for participants of all ages can carry with them lessons that last a lifetime. The lessons young people learn as being part of an organized athletic team, even at the "park and rec" league or "bitty basketball" level, often leave an indelible mark that endures well into adulthood. But what kind of lessons should our kids really be learning as they participate in athletics? Are most coaches at the pre-teen and elementary school level really prepared to teach these lessons to such impressionable young people?

The purpose of the book is to give coaches, parents, and young athletes a "duffle bag" full of the "gear" they need to pursue excellence. It's a combination storybook/coaches' handbook filled with a collection of instructions, stories, illustrations, and anecdotes about the heart, mind, and soul of winners. In short, this book is about the lessons of character development and mental excellence as they can be discovered by players, coaches, and parents alike in the context of sport. The book helps to shape a mindset that continually engages the pursuit of excellence rather than simply allowing the scoreboard to determine victory. Indeed, in building a champion, many tools are required, and they must be handled by serious craftsmen lest their utility be squandered due to lack of focus, inexperience, or intent.

The "duffle bag" is divided into various compartments—coaching or performing themes—each designed to give the reader something to prompt or inspire their thinking and are followed by several concrete application points. Just as a duffle bag contains shorts, t-shirt, and shoes to outfit the athlete for performance, application points become the mental, physical, and spiritual gear—weapons in the arsenal of competitive engagement, all used with the understanding that the game isn't so much played against the opponent as it is against the self.

Also included are applied coaching techniques that help frame the athletic contest as a character-building laboratory. Rather than hoping kids pick up the character lessons from the game, the coach can intentionally educate them through a story or by using an application point in the flow of the game. The book facilitates an intentional way to direct the attention of the coaches, kids, and parents toward positive gains that go far beyond the message of the scoreboard. The coach will have a ready arsenal of messages and techniques that can challenge, inspire, correct, and educate, setting the stage for a cohesive network of parental and community support for the young people involved.

Parents will find this book particularly useful in helping their young performers begin to understand what the pursuit of excellence really means. They can help their kids keep a healthy perspective about the sport experience, balancing the desire for victory with the reality of managing defeat. Parents will have teaching tools and application points with which to prompt their children as they head out the door to practice or to school. In short, the book offers parents a platform for constructive conversation and teaching as they help nurture the development of their children, talking with them about success, failure, mental preparation, and maturity as they experience life's challenges.

SECTION I

A Coaching Foundation: Where It All Begins

The focus of this section is to provide
a brief introduction to the nature of coaching
an athletic team.

1

Managing and Leading

Shepherd the flock of God…which is among you, serving as overseers—not by compulsion, but willingly, not for dishonest gain but eagerly; nor as being lords over those entrusted to you, but being examples to the flock; and when the Chief Shepherd appears, you will receive the crown of glory that does not fade away (1 Peter 5:2-4 NKJV).

Efficient management without effective leadership is like straightening deck chairs on the Titanic.
—Stephen Covey, *The 7 Habits of Highly Effective People*

Youth sports have never been more ripe for Christian coaches that can impact the leaders of tomorrow. Young people desperately need effective adult role models, people who "breathe life" into their young and often turbulent lives, offering hope, guidance, and instruction about success and stability in the midst of chaos. Due in part to the magnetic appeal of athletics, a window of opportunity still exists for young athletes to see a strong role model in their coach.

Our Model for Coaching

Those of us who have coached athletic teams, at any level, know that as a coach we must fulfill many different roles with different task demands, not the least of which is to be a model for our athletes. The example the coach gives his/her team must encompass many things, but first and foremost it must be permeated with integrity and trustworthiness, honesty and respect, and love and hope. The Christian coach, in short, must follow in the footsteps of the greatest coach of all—Jesus.

We see in Jesus a coaching example that includes both management and leadership. On various occasions recorded in the New Testament, Jesus was managing crisis situations, calming distressed people, and training His disciples in the ways of ministry. Other times, He was teaching spiritual principles, pointing the way to godliness and salvation, carrying the banner of faith, hope, and love, and leading lost souls to redemption. Indeed, in Jesus, we see the complete coaching package—*effective management* of physical and human resources along with *effective leadership* following a God-given vision, all the while encompassing a *model of service and obedience* to the glory of the Father.

Indeed, coaches of youth sports must become both managers and leaders. The practical use of physical resources within the program is part of the role of a *manager*— someone who oversees the physical resources and puts them to use. In this role we have many duties: We are responsible for determining the practice schedule, equipment needs, the starting lineup, the travel itinerary and the members of the traveling party, along with a host of details that require precise organizational skills.

The coach's parallel role is that of a *leader*—one who inspires and guides, one who nurtures and unites the spiritual resources of the team, and one who assists the team in deriving its collective identity and purpose—its "meaning." We are also responsible for determining the policies of conduct to which the team will adhere, the overall goals of the program, the principles that guide the program, and the general course of action the team will take en route toward its goals.

While we may be trained to varying degrees in the "X's and O's" of the game, including all kinds of managerial decisions, few of us are truly well-trained for the real leadership of a program—establishing its mission and values. Most of us have never actually considered the "whys" behind the day-to-day decisions of coaching, leaving a gaping hole in the leadership of our team or program. Even if we possess state-of-the-art "know-how," we may be at a loss in the "know-why." Our foremost role as leader is to be the instrument of positive influence, a social architect who designs and builds a vision and purpose for the team, which distinguishes it as a special group.

Significant leadership decisions fundamentally originate in the heart. Therefore, coaching teams to great heights—making a difference in the lives of the players—requires a leader with a great heart. For example, what is the meaning of the word "effort" in your program? Does it simply mean the hustle required to play hard in games and to practice fundamental skills or does it also mean the effort required to be a good learner, self-disciplined, and unselfish?

Leaders must also determine what value and meaning to give events such as winning and losing as they are related to the team and its growth and maturity. They must be able to communicate the importance of these shared values and generate a commitment of the players to the philosophy of the organization.

Leaders are the instruments of change that allow a group's creative and collective efforts to be further blended into something more purposeful. As our teams are taught the meaning behind their collective experience through our consistent reinforcement of proper values, attitudes, and actions, expectations will begin to take root and traditions will be birthed. The vision and purpose will then become the standard by which the program measures success and eventually be an intrinsic part of its tradition. Indeed, the coach sometimes becomes the symbol for the meaning of the program. One only need look at the various traditions in college sports: Phog Allen's influence is still felt at Kansas, Knute Rockne's at Notre Dame, Adolph Rupp's at Kentucky, and John Wooden's at UCLA.

The kind of leadership that unifies and transforms a team involves a special relationship between coach and players and is built on trust, rapport, and mutual values. The result of this leadership effort stands as morally purposeful and elevating when the participants are completely "on board." The meaning of the athletic activity or contest will eventually transcend the game itself.

No doubt you can recall the coach or teacher who somehow communicated to you the important message that you matter, your contributions are important, your attitude impacts others, and your potential is completely unique. As a result, you were able to play a significant role as part of the team or group by aligning your energies behind the team's common goal. If coaching really is more about giving something to others, we must strive to assist others in the same way. And remember, Coach, you can never control what you get, only what you give…

The following is a passage from a 1930 National Education Association (NEA) Journal that crystallizes the substance of leadership:

> No written word, no oral plea
> Can teach our youth what they should be.
> Nor all the books on all the shelves,
> It's what the teachers are themselves.

"TIP-INS" FOR…Managing and Leading
1. Develop excellent communication skills—written and spoken—as well as become purposeful in your actions.
2. Be results-oriented and process-focused—envision the outcome while focusing on the details required to get there.
3. Build trust through a consistent and repetitious example.
4. Treat others as you would like to be treated.
5. Express your willingness to risk failure.
6. Reinforce how the program's guiding principles give meaning to one's actions.

2

Moving From Potential
to Performance

Let your eyes look straight ahead and your eyelids look right before you. Ponder the path of your feet, and let all your ways be established. Do not turn to the right or the left; remove your foot from evil (Prov. 4: 25-27).

As a coach, ask yourself: "At the end of the day, how do I know if I have been successful? Who determines what measuring stick will be used to evaluate me and my team?" Typical means of measuring success might be: the scoreboard, parents, boosters, the media, comparisons to peers, win/loss record, number of players at the next level, athletic directors, and program supervisors. Make no mistake, these are real and very powerful factors, but they are also ones over which we as coaches have little, if any, control.

For example, the scoreboard often doesn't tell the whole story. Moreover, parents are rarely objective, and boosters often have a vested financial interest, making each of them biased critics. The media can only "re-present" events (despite its efforts to create them), peers often make emotional evaluations depending on our relationships with them, and coaching records don't necessarily reflect the quality of an opponent.

In a conversation I had with Hall of Fame coach John Wooden about what makes coaches and leaders great, he shared the following bit of wisdom that captured what I believe to be the essence of great coaching:

Great leaders are always out in front with a banner rather than behind with a whip.

—*John Wooden*

The challenge for us coaches is to make sure we have the right banner.

The Apostle Paul, on the subject of being living examples, admonishes us in Philippians 2:15 to "...shine as lights in the [dark] world." Again, we're challenged to present an example that is illuminating, one that casts light into dark places so that others are drawn to it. Both statements capture an essential leadership concept that inspires rather than cajoles people toward achieving their goals. Coaching kids toward victory means that we must be ready to express (both verbally and non-verbally) what we know is good, right, and important. We must always strive to instill the virtues that made Jesus a successful, battle-tested warrior who walked in faith and was prepared for battle.

Therefore, our coaching must include both words and actions. New Testament author James writes, "You see then that a man is justified by works, and not by faith only" (James 2:24, NKJV). More than merely speaking of the virtues of a champion, we must model these virtues for our players and display them in the heat of battle to move the team from a position of mere potential to a place of success. If we simply say or believe silently that we possess these virtues without demonstrating them to our athletes, two scenarios arise: 1) our actions will become the living testimony they will follow more than our words, and 2) we will lose credibility as coaches, compromising both the ability of the team to realize its full potential and our authority as leaders of the team.

Every coach has a potential both for good and for bad so let's not be deceived about our capacity to influence the time either way. While many teams have had great talent, some of them failed to realize their potential, despite their superior skills, because of their leadership. Knowing we have potential is one thing—using it is quite another.

Successful programs, like successful people, emphasize the competence and character needed to resist mediocrity and pursue God's best. This fundamental combination of body, mind, and spirit unified in truth unlocks the true spirit of champions. Putting too much stock in potential without demanding its end result is a dangerous condition. Indeed, we have God-given skills, talents, and abilities, and we are called to make the most of them and use them in the service of the Lord, working for God and not for man. As it says in

Matthew 5:15: "Neither do people light a lamp and put it under a bowl. Instead they put it on its stand, and it gives light to everyone in the house." We must use our potential and our words to make a difference.

Vision and Purpose

With these things in mind, if our players and programs are going to mature, there are three important considerations for us to consider: 1) Is there a vision for our program? 2) Is there a sense of purpose for our team? and 3) What are the principles that will shape the conduct both on and off the field of play? Vision, purpose, and good principles determine how far we can move our team from mere potential toward successful performance. Indeed, these are the things which we as coaches have some direct control over and are given the powerful opportunity to instill into our kids.

When we consistently communicate the vision, both in spoken word and in deed, our players and programs have a clear aim at reaching success rather than at merely avoiding failure. Our players and programs become oriented toward "playing to win" instead of "playing not to lose." (Of course each program is different, and each age group must be addressed differently and will take away a different degree of the principles you share with them.)

Vision

1. *Share the vision often.* Tell the people in your program about your genuine belief in their ability to make something special happen—there is a difference between a dream and a fantasy. Paint a realistic picture for them about what you

want the program to look like when they leave or when your work in the program is complete. Enthusiasm and passion are contagious. If you are consistent and sincere, and the cause is bigger than one person, they will follow.

2. *Challenge the staff and players to set a new standard of quality.* Encourage them to do what they do a little bit better than they've done it before. Stress consistency in each aspect of their lives so they can balance academics, athletics, faith, and family. Reinforce the notions of personal improvement and self-discipline. After all, only the individual really knows if they've been successful. Be demanding, but never dehumanizing.

3. *Be willing to risk failure.* Give your program the freedom to fail as well as the freedom to succeed. This freedom removes their constant fear of rejection and isolation. In pursuit of one's vision, people are likely to get into uncharted territory, which means they must learn how to adjust. And with learning comes trial and error, which we need to see not as failure, only feedback. If the players are struggling, that's good because it means they're moving up.

Purpose

1. *Establish a mission for yourself and for your program.* At the end of the day, we should be able to hold up our activities beside the mission and see precisely how they fit. The more activities that are directly linked to a sense of purpose, the more consistent and effective the performance will become. Commit it to paper and give it meaning by con-

necting the players' performance to the purpose included in the mission statement. If your players can't recite the mission statement of the team off the top of their heads, it either doesn't mean anything to them or it may be too wordy or fuzzy in concept.

2. *Foster accountability.* As a team, the group must be unified in its pursuit of excellence. The group is collectively responsible for its activity, both on and off the court. Individuals will contribute differently, but each one has an equal responsibility to give everything they have toward the betterment of the team. Accountability means that they must answer for how well their performance or attitude fits with the team's overall purpose and mission. This only happens in an environment of trust and humility, when the team is dedicated to a sense of purpose that goes far beyond the pettiness of liking or disliking one another. Accountability breeds respect of teammates and promotes an inner sense of decency in helping the others.

3. *Use quotes, illustrations and stories as teaching tools.* These teaching tools must be used to create reflective and engaging thought about one's role in fulfilling the mission of the team or about the journey toward excellence. Trophy cases and championship banners are visual symbols of past successes. Stories of former players are often another way to connect people with a sense of purpose and tradition. A quick story or quote, thoughtfully examined by the team at the start of practice, can prepare the mind and heart for a spirited workout.

4. *Make the most of teachable moments.* Let people know when they're on target and correct them when they are not. Practice time is certainly for action, but, most importantly, it's the best time for teaching and learning. As Coach Wooden has said, "Never mistake activity for achievement." You may succeed in teaching something by stopping the action and using an illustration or story rather than rushing on to the next drill. Keep in mind what your coaching activities are ultimately trying to achieve. Remember the mission...

Principles

1. *Identify five trademark words, cue words that will guide your program in every aspect.* These are words such as unity, respect, self-discipline, and unselfishness that can be used to describe performance as well as other aspects of life, such as going to class, loaning a friend your truck, paying for someone else's lunch, or simply giving your time to someone who needs it. These words and their meaning become the direct link to the coach's beliefs about what really matters. These words, over time, become the unspoken code of behavior that will guide the program on and off the court.

2. *Emphasize these principles with your example.* The way in which these principles are communicated by adults is essential to their being adopted by the young players. To be effective, the principles must be "caught" as they are observed in the program's leadership as well as taught again and again during a time of instruction. For example, create a positive energy around the concept of not only being first,

but also being best. Again, accountability and consequence, both positive and negative, enhance the likelihood these principles will be used by staff and players for a long, long time.

3. *Stand firm.* In selecting principles, be sure they are something you truly believe will make a difference in your team. They will no doubt be challenged, and you will be called upon to uphold them. Just as Paul exhorted the Ephesians, you also put on the full armor of God, for you will surely be tested. "Therefore put on the full armour of God, so that when the day of evil comes, you may be able to stand your ground, and after you have done everything, to stand" (Eph. 6:13). If you don't truly think a principle is worth fighting for, there is not much of a chance that it will have any lasting positive impact on the players or the program. If you don't believe in it, why should your players?

4. *Be consistent.* Coaches must be both tough and compassionate at the same time. Remember when it's time to dole out discipline, it's the action you don't approve of, not the person who did it. For that reason, your toughness and consistency must be tempered with a full understanding that you have received many second chances in life. When arriving at decisions, recall the words of Abraham Lincoln when he was criticized for his perceived inaction during the Civil War, "I may walk slowly, but I never walk back."

Certainly one can be compassionate and firm at the same time—it's called "tough love." Treat others as you would like to be treated. "Be quick to listen and slow to speak and become angry" as it says in James 1:19.

To march out in front with a banner can be scary because everyone will observe and evaluate, praise or criticize, and accept or reject. Yet there are two things I have learned in coaching: 1) Most people don't know what it takes to truly be successful, and 2) If they do know what it takes, most of them aren't willing to do it.

Because youth sports are in desperate need of strong leaders and strong role models, each of us has an opportunity today to raise a banner for Jesus and everything He represents. Instead of cajoling and coddling the elusive trappings of victory, let us boldly pursue, with renewed passion, the educational essence of coaching. In the process, may we model for young people the time-tested principles that have always resulted in enduring excellence. And in the end, each of us can take pride in knowing we did our best to help others become the best they were capable of becoming.

"TIP-INS" FOR...Moving from Potential to Performance
1. The law of the harvest applies—good things take time to grow and mature.
2. "Potential" is a dangerous word when not used carefully. When applied to some, it's a "lift"; for others, it's a "weight."
3. "Stay the course" once you've articulated vision, mission, goals, and values because young performers crave stability as they learn and mature.
4. Be willing to do things other coaches or parents might not be willing to do by taking time to write out the "game plan" of the team or program—be a banner carrier!

3

Setting People Up for Success

For physical training is of some value, but godliness has value for all things, holding promise for both the present life and the life to come" (1 Tim. 4:8).

When I think about the truly satisfying elements of coaching, I think about those exciting times when players "get it." Their eyes light up, they break into a big grin, run a little faster, and jump a little higher, knowing that they just learned something really neat. At those times, the physical training pays off, and the work getting there was worth it. As coaches, we work and work to encourage young people in their progress, and when they finally claim success for themselves, there isn't much better than this moment! We know we coached them to the point of success, and they "got it"!

I wonder how Jesus feels when we respond to His loving acts of coaching and truly "get it." Jesus spent much time teaching his rag-tag ensemble of disciples, constantly moving them closer to understanding who He was and what He was doing, believing in them by demonstrating His unending love. Jesus kept the mission foremost in His mind and began growing His disciples up in the faith that they might lead others. In the same way, a great coach will see the possibility in each of the players and then help them achieve it.

Just as effective teaching is sometimes about asking questions that lead to responses down a certain line, so too is coaching. Coaches create drills and activities that allow their players to discover deeper understandings of the game's mechanics. Most of us are constantly on the lookout for ways to help our young players experience successful performance and improvement. As Paul reminded Timothy, the physical training is fine, but training that leads to godliness is best. It is our coaching challenge today, too, because it gives the person a foundation upon which to act.

Think through some of the examples in the New Testament for a moment. How many times did Jesus do something the disciples could not understand? In their confusion, they needed for Him to explain what happened because they had missed His point. Jesus wasn't performing the miracles solely for His disciples' development, but He was training them. As His disciples matured, Jesus pushed them just a little bit further in their faith, constantly aware of how far they could go, yet never pushing them beyond the brink. Jesus continues to constantly set up His people for success as we obey and follow.

Effective team leaders have long been recognized for their abilities to make the rest of the team perform as a unit: for example, to "set the other players up" by getting the ball to the ones in a position to score, thereby assisting the coach on the floor or on the field. It's not only the coach but also the point guard who unselfishly makes players on the basketball court perform better by getting people into positions to be effective and successful. The concept of "setting others up for success" is really about being a servant. Jesus dismantled the selfish mindset of self-aggrandizement that so many coaches are intoxicated with today by saying, "Not so with you. Instead, whoever wants to become great among you must be your servant" (Mark 10:43). In short, the essence of coaching is servant leading.

Success

What, then, is success? For Christ-centered coaches and athletes, the focus should be on each team member's improvement, not just physically and mentally, but also spiritually toward godliness. The mindset should be on the one thing the individual can ever hope to control—themselves. No comparisons to others are required in order to assess this type of improvement. In the heart of a champion, success is a single-minded effort to make the most out of one's own God-given talents and abilities, rather than in concerning oneself with someone else's skills or actions.

The real challenge in coaching for this type of success is in the practical matter of actually getting athletes to "buy in" to this idea. The secret to its accomplishment lies in: 1) knowing your players, and 2) forthright communication.

When you know your players well, you can properly and meaningfully motivate and challenge them. If you don't really know your players as individuals, you can only use guesswork when you try to hit their "hot buttons." No wonder Jesus is so effective—He knows His "players" inside and out. And in spite of our pathetic performances, He keeps coaching us anyway, setting us up with chance after chance, many more than we rightfully deserve.

Communication lays the foundation of relationship so that the applied motivation is understood as being in the best interest of the person(s) involved. The player/coach relationship is about providing an environment where people are free to pursue excellence at the highest levels while simultaneously possessing the freedom to fail, without loss of personal dignity or esteem, because of the pervading love and camaraderie. When we give our players the freedom to succeed *and* the freedom to fail—without compromising on the quality of effort—there is no failure, but only feedback complete with suggestions for improvement.

Creating an environment dedicated to excellence is liberating, but it also carries with it a tremendous responsibility for the participants because there can be no excuses for lack of effort, focus, or commitment. With empowerment comes responsibility, and young performers, as well as coaches and parents, must realize that if their kids are to begin climbing the ladder to lofty achievements, each contributing person must become responsible for their own journey and their own behaviors.

Coaches represent a safety net. In case the young eagles aren't quite ready to get out of the nest but decide to try anyway, coaches are there to correct, encourage, and comfort them with the attitude of facilitating interdependence rather than dependence. Key ingredients in this interdependent environment are trust, mutual respect between player and coach, discipline, patience, and a spiritual readiness for "rough and tumble."

Athletics, like life, are all about learning, and with learning comes a fair amount of trial and error, and of course, success. Setting people up for success means leading them toward getting just a little bit better than they were yesterday without them recognizing that you had anything to do with it. The disciples knew there was something special about Jesus, but they didn't fully get it, even as He was performing miracles. They didn't realize the magnitude of their relationship with Him until after He had ascended to heaven.

The brief time coaches spend with the kids on their team may be the only exposure some of them will have to the love of Jesus. Though you might not see success right away, trust that they will appreciate you more as they grow older and mature. Set them up for success and let the Lord "seal the deal" in His time and in His way.

"TIP-INS" FOR...Setting People Up for Success

1. The concept is like an assist—an opportunity for someone else created by your unselfish act.
2. Use goals which focus on the process of improvement rather than the end product.
3. Target individual attitudes and efforts—they are the only elements under direct control of the individual athlete.
4. As leader, be motivated by an attitude of unselfishness bathed in faith, hope, and love.
5. Keep perspective...you can lead a horse to water, but you can't make it think.

4

Unique People

[Jesus said,] *My command is this: Love one another as I have loved you* (John 15:12).

Consider for a moment the plight of our coaching colleague, Kathy, a rookie coach just beginning to learn the ropes…

Kathy was amazed as she met with her soccer team. The realization struck her as she began watching the girls warm-up before their first practice. *All these 7th graders from the same town—but no two are approaching this practice session in exactly the same way,* she thought. As a new and inexperienced head coach, Kathy, the volunteer and community servant, found herself soberly considering how she would begin to take command of her team, earn the respect of the athletes, be fair, and keep everyone's parents happy. *First things first,* she resolved, and decided to put the girls first, for the time being.

There were 35 girls on the field waiting for Kathy to begin giving them direction and instruction. Some were left-footed; some were right-footed. Some were working with a partner; others were working alone. Some simply stood and watched the others while still others mingled together to socialize, not entirely certain whether they should be talking to each other, kicking a ball back and forth, or running wind sprints. Where would Kathy begin?

There is no truer maxim in athletic programs for young kids than the expression, "Everybody's different." We're always reminded of this when we consider the concept of "team" and how we are supposed to bring dissimilar individuals into a common group with common values and beliefs. Jesus was also challenged by this, and always worked against the notion that some groups were privileged while others were condemned. In addition, Jesus went so far as to "call out" the "pretenders" in the faith from the "contenders"—the real believers. We find a similar challenge in coaching today.

It seems like young athletes, in their search for belonging, oftentimes take on a persona of someone they've seen on TV. If they can just act like a particular player, the they hope that maybe others will think they really are like that player. The "wanna-be's" hope to be admitted into the select circle of great players who receive a lot of playing time and attention. They've succumbed to the notion that it's best to look good and pretend when you don't really know something. It seems more rational for them to get caught pretending to be someone rather than to admit you're no one.

As members of the athletic culture, we have been poor examples for the young players because we have set up our own façades of strength and bravado—the stuff that we believe signals dominance, superiority, and success. Take a look

22

at our colleagues, fellow coaches, players, and their parents. Indeed, let's take a good look at ourselves. If we're truly objective, it won't take long to see the "winner" façade visible in the workout or coaching gear we wear, in the way we speak to our players, and in the way we carry ourselves on the sidelines. Indeed, many coaches would sooner copy what they *think* is right than to copy what they *know* is right. They rationalize that if it works for the college and professional teams on TV, then it ought to work for eleven year-olds! "Facade coaching" turns opportunity into a scary four-letter word, one that most young athletes are ill-equipped to handle—risk! If we, like our young athletes, don't measure up to the criteria by winning more games, then we fear others will write us off as losers; while, in reality, we should be committed to more important goals than merely scoring more points than the other team.

Do you find yourself coaching conditionally by giving preferential treatment only to those who can throw the long pass, jump the highest, or hit the best? If the goal is only to win, then the response is easy. However, in God's eyes, we're all pretenders and "wanna-be's," fallen people who may or may not be ready to admit we are woefully inadequate in the game of life and need His unconditional coaching in our lives.

Therefore, we must be ready to accept the young athletes unconditionally just as God has done for us. When they sense our total acceptance, the players will feel free to admit that they truly need to work hard to improve. It is only then that we will see real progress in their lives, both on and off the field.

Building a Team Out of Diversity

Each player has radically different idiosyncrasies that make them tick. Some players are soft-spoken, and some are loud and gregarious. Some are silly, and some are serious. Some exude a brash and swashbuckling attitude when they compete, while others are the quiet warriors with a fire that always burns deep and hot. On each new team we are confronted with a group of young people in which no two are exactly the same—and truth be told, we wouldn't want it any other way.

Building a team involves far more than merely assembling a group of people with a common interest in a sport. We're constantly challenged with the ever-changing task of figuring out how to motivate each one; first gaining their respect and then facilitating their development as an athlete and as a person.

Having a blanket set of motivation practices or team rules doesn't really make sense since players come to us with unique personalities, physical capabilities, backgrounds, and records—in short, the combination of each one is different. It is easy to generalize player attributes into patterns in an attempt to formulate one rule that fits everyone. But as easy as it may be for us to make assumptions about a young person and begin treating them in a manner consistent with these assumptions, it may be exactly the wrong and unfair basis from which to begin coaching them.

The coaching challenges seem to multiply when we consider treating athletes individually on a case-by-case basis. Athletes, coaches, and parents like the "one size fits all" perspective because, on the surface, it appears to reduce ambi-

24

guity, but in reality it does not. If we have a team rule that says: "If a person misses a practice, they don't play one entire game," it fits nice and clean, because the inappropriate behavior is so clearly laid out. But what about the kid who was required to stay home take care of her little brother in a family emergency and was unable to contact you—does the rule still apply? No two kids or scenarios are exactly the same, meaning that each one should be treated as unique since there are exceptions to every man-made rule.

There is nothing wrong with team rules, although generally I would recommend the fewer the better. Naturally, each athlete is going to bring "a different package to the party," and the only way we find out what's under the wrapping paper is to take the time to unwrap the container and see who is inside. But the key is to always keep a team orientation while focusing on personal performance—always helping young people consider, "How does my attitude and actions impact others?"

Although everyone is different, the uniqueness of the individual must not come at the expense of others, particularly in a team sport. Using a mission statement as a guide, the code of conduct will emerge as the coach teaches and reinforces it, helping players hold up their own behavior to determine if it fits with the overall scheme of what the team is trying to achieve.

Recall we left Kathy with her hands full, wondering how she would start with all those girls. Being clear and direct on the principles of the team will help Kathy carve out the boundaries of attitudes, actions, and performance for the team. Several of the athletes, despite our best attempts at guidance and support, will choose to quit. There simply isn't much we can do for them.

For the majority, however, many athletic teams focus on four primary areas, each possessing a depth of substance that when applied properly can transform a group of seemingly different members into one body: 1) respect, 2) team work, 3) self-discipline, and 4) commitment. Activities or behaviors that place team members outside these guiding principles become distractions and get in the way of progress. Kathy will find that the role of coaching (like parenting) in these four areas not only facilitates good decisions in each area and demands compliance when appropriate, but also teaches and nurtures appropriate development for long-term self discipline and direction.

The overarching concern for coaches is to see each player as an end in themselves rather than simply a means to an end for the coach or someone else to use in order to reach one of their own goals.

"TIP-INS" FOR...Unique People

1. Treat others as you would like to be treated.
2. Be consistent on principles, but flexible in their application.
3. Find ways to capitalize on players' uniquenesses by utilizing them in productive ways toward team goals.
4. The surest way to be partial is to treat everyone the same—they're not all the same.
5. There still is no "I" in "team." This fact won't be changing anytime soon.
6. Consider the wisdom of Benjamin Franklin, who said as he met with the other Founding Fathers, "Surely we must all stand together, or else we will all hang separately."

5

Trust and Credibility

Since we have these promises, dear friends, let us purify ourselves from everything that contaminates body and spirit, perfecting holiness out of reverence for God (2 Cor. 7:1).

What do you suppose happens in the mind of a young athlete when a coach breaks a promise? Jesus reminds us to, "Simply let your 'Yes' be 'Yes' and your 'No', 'No'; anything beyond this comes from the evil one" (Matt. 5:37). Remember when you were a kid, and mom or dad said that the family would go to the ice cream shop after supper but then changed their mind later and said: "It's too late to go now…it's time for bed…"?

When a coach informs a young player that she should get ready to go in the game only to never put her in, it may appear on the outside to be a small matter, a casual oversight, or a misunderstanding. But truth-telling and promise keeping are perhaps even more important to impressionable young athletes than to adults. Whereas adults may possess the maturity to understand various imperfections in other people, young people see models like coaches, teachers, and parents as moral reference points of stability and security, and when these are compromised, the feelings of betrayal sometimes last a lifetime.

Trust and credibility may be the two most important character attributes we can bring to our teams. In a sense, our credibility rests in our ability to be trusted. Trust is an interpersonal currency with which people conduct the day's affairs and where one's trustworthiness determines the value of the currency. To the extent that coaching is about high-performance/high-expectation relationships, establishing trust and credibility represent the essence of our educational endeavor as coaches—encouraging athletes to become vulnerable in their relationships with us and trust us as coaches to treat and train them properly. This is no lighthearted task because, after all, we're dealing with a child who is someone else's most loved and most valuable possession. So, for an athlete to express a willingness to be challenged toward greater improvement, they first have to open the door to the coach's emotional and psychological access to them.

For instance, if the base runner wants to get to second base from first, they must first make an unreserved commitment to the action of running to second base, making themselves a target between places of safety. In the absence of trust and credibility (in their own skills, in this case), the base runner never finds the confidence to run freely when he/she doesn't trust his/her own abilities to steal the base. Will the outcome likely be successful?

Likewise, without these two attributes of trust and credibility in the player/coach/parent relational triad, young athletes will very seldom make themselves vulnerable enough to "put it all on the line," either in their commitment to the coach or in their commitment to their own performance. The gains (in the mind of the athlete) never outweigh the risk, especially if the child is unsure of who they are and what they can do. Isn't the essence of success in sport a maximum effort in the complete deployment of mind, body, and spirit toward realizing a goal? How can a person or team set their sights on a successful future if everyone is constantly looking over their shoulders, distracted by the task of "protecting their back"? Emotional safety and security in the young person's relationship to the coach is essential. How reassuring was it for Joshua when God informed him, "I'll never leave nor forsake you"? (Jos 1:5) That's real security indeed!

John Wooden shared with me the notion of trust and credibility for coaches:

—•••—

If you're honest and straightforward with people, you'll never have to remember what you've said.

—John Wooden

—•••—

Wooden's gems of insightful wisdom address what management gurus Jim Kouzes and Barry Posner describe as "d-w-y-s-y-w-d" or "doing what you say you will do" (Kouzes and Posner, 1993). Herein lies a principle that goes well beyond athletics, parenting, business, or any other performance endeavor.

When applied to athletics, trust and credibility are vital. The competitive arena of sports itself is a powder keg loaded with the explosive agents of high visibility, media scrutiny, and high levels of expectation and intensity that, when mixed together, could yield great achievement or intense disappointment. Indeed, trust and credibility must be in place for a team to respond to virtually instantaneous adversity or challenge. Competition brings such unpredictability that often times there is no time to call "time out" and regroup, but only time to act and respond. The team must be physically, emotionally, and spiritually secure and mature in themselves and in their relationships to each other, particularly the coach, if they are to respond successfully at a moment's notice.

How to Gain Credibility

Gaining trust and credibility seems equally simple yet tensely complex. Relating to other people should not be all that difficult with some basic people skills. Yet when high achievers, with lofty goals and ambitions, commit their wonderful God-given abilities and talents to work in pursuit of those goals, personal agendas often seem to become more important than the good of the team, and relationships get strained under the pressure to win.

Human nature has a tendency to place the needs of self well above the needs of others. But we can choose another path, one embracing the notions of teamwork and unselfishness, selflessness and humility, making trust and credibility matters of primary concern rather than secondary options in our relations with other people. Some have twisted team work into meaning that the team is in place so that an individual can "showcase" his/her talent while others get them the ball. In these cases, when the role of the team is to help the one rather than to help each other, the mission of the team is ignored.

This kind of attitude among players points to an interesting challenge for coaches in the character development process. Clearly we coaches play an important role, but no more or no less important a role than any other adult associated with the athletic experience available to a young person. The significance of the relationship between player and coach is huge, but the importance for all adults to be good character role models is no more or less than it is for the coach.

Kids need to "see" character in *all* the adults involved, each working together to communicate the value in the many "teachable moments" so readily available in athletics. Servant-leading or "servant-coaching" must stem out of an attitude of humility; otherwise young athletes will quickly see through the veil of false pretense to the coach's ego and self-serving agenda. In this kind of disposition, we all find exhortation in the Apostle Paul's challenge, "Do nothing out of selfish ambition or vain conceit, but in humility consider others better than yourselves" (Phil. 2:3).

The "how" of actually relating with others represents those moments in which many players and parents form their sense of whether they will give trust or suspicion, whether they will reject or accept the leader, and whether they will "buy in" or hold out from accepting the vision and purpose of the team. Most of us aren't used to seeing humility truly played out in the midst of an athletic contest. When players, fellow coaches, parents, team organizers, and others take it upon themselves to lead their lives in a humble, trustworthy, and honest way, it frees the team environment from the plague of second-guessing, hidden agendas, and innuendo—all not-so-affectionately referred to as "mind games." When relating to a humble coach, our players are free from constantly having to occupy their minds with the task of trying to sort out what was really meant by another person's comments or behaviors.

Perhaps those of us in leadership positions would benefit by broadening our own sense of perspective and being careful not to make promises we can't or don't intend to keep. We must model a goal-oriented lifestyle, a great work ethic and dedication, and a willingness to press on in the face of adversity. Still, we must be mindful of how our actions and our beliefs impact our relationships with those persons with whom we work, live, and perform. In the words of Emerson, the 19th century American philosopher, "What you're doing speaks so loudly I cannot hear what you are saying." The character of the coach matters.

Reference

Kouzes, J. & Posner, B. (1993). *Credibility: How leaders gain it and lose it, why people demand it.* San Francisco, CA: Jossey Bass Publishers.

"TIP-INS" FOR...Trust and Credibility
1. Tell the truth—honesty remains the best policy and people respect "straight talk."

2. Trust and credibility, once lost, are virtually impossible to restore. Try to never damage your own credibility.

3. Use tact and sensitivity when communicating difficult messages to young people. Being told the truth, even if it isn't good news, is better than being the victim of disrespect by having been lied to.

4. If you are going to "do what you say you will do," choose very carefully what you say to your team, because you then must do it.

SECTION II

LEADING THE TEAM

The focus of this section is to highlight
the basic leadership elements that are associated
with coaching, making sure that the values, goals,
and general sense of mission for the team or
program are consistent and appropriate.

6

Being a Student of Your Own Game

We do not dare to classify or compare ourselves with some who commend themselves. When they measure themselves by themselves and compare themselves with themselves, they are not wise (2 Cor. 10:4).

Isn't it interesting how we seek benchmarks in everything we do? Coaching is no different. We are always on the lookout for indicators to determine how we measure up in comparison to other coaches and always find some who are better than we are and some who are not as fortunate. Finding someone who's not quite as successful somehow satisfies us and makes us feel that we really are accomplishing something. But seeing those who are achieving more than we do tends to keep us on our toes.

The Apostle Paul advised us to "work out our salvation with fear and trembling..." (Phil 2: 12) Here Paul is challenging us to never become complacent in the faith, to continue striving to emulate the model that Jesus gave us. As we continue to mature in the faith, we recognize our flaws and weaknesses, and realize that the road Jesus wants us to follow is long, and we have only begun down the path. In essence, we must become students of ourselves and of our faith journey.

This same principle in coaching of always striving to learn more (which we also pass down to the players) helps us to maintain focus, not on our achievements, but on the process of growth and maturity. Legendary UCLA men's basketball coach John Wooden said it this way:

It's what you learn

after you know it all

that counts.

—*John Wooden*

I believe he's right. Once we've come to the saving knowledge of Jesus and accepted his salvation, we know the essence of the Gospel, but there is so much more that Jesus wants to reveal in our lives that the moment we get complacent and choose to place our focus on other things, we cease to move forward, and our faith stagnates. And, just as is the case in our spiritual walk, if we stop honing our coaching skills, we stop improving.

For many of us, we have accepted Jesus as Lord and Savior just as we have accepted the fact that we know something about a particular sport that we coach in a rather common and matter of fact way. Salvation has become familiar like an old pair of workout shoes. At this point, the joy of salvation that David longed for (Ps. 51:12) and the joy we experienced when we first met Jesus, becomes mundane and taken for granted. The result is that we drift into mediocrity and become a vessel of warfare the enemy considers disengaged and therefore not a threat to him. We find ourselves comfortable in our knowledge and assurance that we can achieve goals, both personal and professional—and our complacency slowly draws us to a stop, either because we have deceived ourselves into thinking we have all the information we need or we have failed to realize the vital necessity of constant learning and growth. In "coach-speak," either we're getting better or we're getting worse...there is no middle.

As a result, we fail to realize that in spite of our confidence and our significant forward progress to-date, that there is still so much more to know and understand. The notion eludes us that we must continue working, learning, growing, and challenging ourselves to stringent standards of improvement. We don't feel guilty if we miss our daily time in the Word, skip our time of prayer, or permit ourselves a moment of self-indulgence. It's in those moments that we are vulnerable to spiritual attack, and our vigorous pursuit of excellence slows to a casual saunter...

Training for a Champion

For many coaches, any coaching preparation received in college is barely an introduction and certainly nothing that aids the Christian coach in developing a knowledge of how to impart the real heart of a champion. Whether or not the coach has any classroom training or occasional practicum study, the "real" coaching education arguably begins when actually working with young athletes. The nuances of coaching, only acquired through experience, seem endless to the beginner, and even more elusive to the coaching veteran. Yet, when mastered through patient study and vigilant dedication, they become the difference between teams that reach their potential and those that only get close.

Being a coach is seldom easy, but it can be fun. The practical principles of coaching along with the intricacies of interpersonal human relationships as they present themselves in athletics include a host of challenging, interesting, and confounding aspects that make coaching one of the most exciting and rewarding activities in life.

These principles are affected by your teaching style and communication techniques that influence whether or not you present new materials effectively and efficiently. We know that repetition is the "mother of learning," but effective communication is the glue that helps the repetitions stick together and accumulate. And so you learn that some players learn best by listening, others by seeing, and still others by doing. Without your taking time to understand these needs of the players, as well as your own strengths as a communicator, you'll constantly be wondering why some of the kids aren't able to "get it right." I've learned that when my teams aren't "getting it," it's usually not their fault, but rather it's mine. Individuals who have learned how to train themselves on the job, in the position of coach, are often the ones who progressively rise and sustain levels of coaching excellence.

In learning to listen with your heart as well as your head under the direction of the Holy Spirit, we become sensitized to the spiritual subtleties of coaching that helps us connect with the team at the "heart-level" as well as the "head-level." Coaching "from the heart" is almost a lost art form in modern day coaching, but it can be learned by understanding that the past experiences you've had in life are your preparation for His service, and by your imparting those spiritual life-lessons to the team. The key to unlock performance may not be physical at all, but more probably spiritual through attaining a "fighting spirit" or the "heart of a champion." So we coaches need to communicate to our young players nuggets of wisdom through teaching the principles of God's Word, personalized by our life's application—the lessons of both "head" and "heart."

Roy Williams could represent an example of someone who has become a student of his own coaching. Coach Williams has publicly stated he owes his coaching success to Coach Dean Smith. Even so, he has also stated that Coach Smith's best advice to him when he took the Kansas University men's basketball job was, "Be yourself." For all of the learning Coach Williams did while at North Carolina as an assistant, studying Coach Smith's masterful coaching, he has since been challenged to find ways to make all those teachings his own, to take the North Carolina philosophies and personalize them, first to Kansas, and now back to North Carolina. Coach Williams' growth as a coach came as a result of studying the effects of his own coaching techniques and skills on his players, not Coach Smith's. To Coach Williams' great credit, he has been masterful as a head coach, remaining humble and continuing to deflect credit for his success toward Coach Smith, all while continuing to learn and improve in both the art and science of coaching.

So where might a coach find the energy to do "self-training" and keep the team going at the same time? A good friend and mentor of mine, Rear Admiral Stanton J. Thompson, U.S. Navy Reserve, explained to me that, in many ways, the energy required to stay a step ahead of the opposing side becomes a habitual mindset, borne of the desire to consistently achieve at the highest levels. Admiral Thompson explained that, for him, this sense of motivation to lead in an excellent way comes from three ideas: 1) a sense of competition, 2) a sense of personal pride, and 3) a sense of duty. Admiral Thompson's leadership expertise and insight, gathered throughout over 20 years of association with the U.S. Navy, closely describes the kind of convictions and principles many championship coaches have embraced. And as the coach is growing and improving, the team will naturally reap the reward.

The intentional desire to actively develop our individual skills as coaches enables us to become better coaches. The same applies in our faith walk with Jesus. We must be "coachable," willing to critically look at our own game to see if there is room for improvement, and if there is, to find ways to get better. We can sense the competition of spiritual warfare, the sense of satisfaction in knowing our Lord is pleased when we seek and honor Him with our whole hearts, and we can feel the sense of duty and obligation as servants.

This personal pursuit of "servanthood greatness" represents the challenge within the challenge of coaching. No one can specifically tell you how to get better—each of us must become students of our own coaching, submitted to the counsel of the Holy Spirit for guidance and instruction.

The constant learning process is a great challenge and one that great coaches and leaders take seriously; indeed, they relish it. Rather than trying to clone ourselves into one of sport's great coaches, we need to come to know who we are in Christ, using our own talents, our own skills, and our own "game," and submitting it all to the Lordship of Jesus, the inventor of coaching.

"TIP-INS" FOR...Being a Student of Your Own Game
1. Getting better as a player or a coach requires constant learning.
2. We're not consumed by the activity, only by the desire to be at God's best in the activity.
3. If you're in a committed learning mode, you don't have time for self-aggrandizement because your orientation is one of humility, openly expressing that you don't have all the answers and are actively seeking them.
4. God honors hearts that are humble and "coachable" before Him.
5. Ask questions...Listen...Read...Work Hard

7

The Coach's Motivation

The heart is deceitful above all things and beyond cure.
Who can understand it? 'I the Lord search the heart
and examine the mind, to reward a man according to
his conduct, according to what his deeds deserve' (Jer.
17: 9-10).

What motivates us as coaches to make the decisions we
make? Some would say coaches are motivated by external
sources, like trophies or other material gain. Others would
say they are motivated by internal sources, like the contents
of the heart and soul. I would guess that if we strip away the
veneer, we could agree that most coaching decisions concerning the weightiest matters in our programs are affairs of
the heart. There is something deep in our hearts—a passion—that sets the stage for our most significant and meaningful decisions in life.

We speak so often about teams or athletes competing
with "heart," but what's in the Christian's competitive character that's so special and seemingly intangible? Indeed, as
born-again believers in Christ, the last "game" has already
been won, so how can we lose?

At some point, we need to ask ourselves if our desire to coach, along with our coaching behavior, has anything to do with pleasing God. Let's look at the Apostle Paul for a minute.

Paul's heart was cemented to the goal of becoming Christ-like. Even as he sat facing death in a Philippian jail, beaten and bleeding, his passion for what he was doing remained steadfast, and he was secure in his purpose with his motivation never in doubt. But let's be clear—the old Paul had died on the road to Damascus when his deceitful heart was struck a mortal blow in Christ. As Paul was filled with the Holy Spirit, he became a new man, and the old passed away. Paul's heart began to beat in sync with the rhythm of the Holy Spirit. He was transformed from the inside out, and his walk hit stride with the cadence of his Savior. With Christ as his motivation, he was not only able to achieve greatness in his apostolic adventures, but he was also able to endure harsh and undeserved punishment. He continued to press ahead, suffering what seemed to be (for the casual observer) far more losses than victories. What did he possess that kept him going? It was his passion to serve Jesus with his goal being Christ-likeness.

This kind of inner fire is a pivotal point that players need to hear repeatedly from the coach. Openness about our coaching motives to our players becomes the basis for consistency in expectations and relationships. It is from this foundation that players have a solid reference point about how to interpret our actions. Will we make mistakes? Sure. But as we humble ourselves, making ourselves accountable to Jesus, we allow the Spirit to work through us and restore whatever wrongs may have occurred.

We must recognize and express to the players that the decisions we make are not always right, but most definitely are made with the right motivations as we understand them in Jesus. We must take whatever means necessary to maintain trust and credibility by genuinely expressing the contents of our hearts before our players, particularly when difficult decisions must be made and the climate is ripe among the players for mistrust and innuendo.

It is vital that we stress to our players the checkpoints we use for shaping coaching decisions, each checkpoint linked to the others. Yours may vary, but three checkpoints I've adopted involve developing: 1) good people (character), 2) good players (competency), and 3) good competitors (competitiveness). These overlap, to be sure, but they offer concrete points for young players to "hook into" and become trademark elements of your team. In addition, these checkpoints are the basis from which we formulate decisions related to individual team members and the team as a whole. In short, they become a "bulleted mission statement" for the coach and the team.

As our players learn to appreciate our motives and see our living testimony before them, lines of communication open, encouraging dialogue about a bigger picture for each individual team member. Trust is built and security is established when our purpose is clear and our standards are unchanging. We must operate with a principled foundation to make decisions while, at the same time, allowing players input through dialogue. The healthy understanding between our players and our assistant coaches is the result of a defined relationship between us all whereby a coach may be wrong but most certainly is interested in the well-being of player. Our decisions don't have to be perfect, but we must be humble before the Lord.

Much like families, if players believe in our principled foundation and concept of open dialogue and have repeatedly witnessed our example of striving to fulfill them, they can live with a bad, poor, or flat-out wrong decision. Most importantly, they will be willing to at least listen to our explanation, since they understand we are motivated by the right reasons.

"TIP-INS" FOR...The Coach's Motivation
1. Build relationships of trust through honest and consistent player/coach interactions.
2. Use individual meetings to discuss the bigger picture related to individuals becoming 1) good people, 2) good players, and 3) good competitors.
3. Give yourself the freedom to fail along with the freedom to succeed in making coaching decisions—it's impossible to be perfect, this side of heaven. If your heart is truly right, your players will understand.
4. If your heart is in Christ, coach from your heart.

8

Achieving More
May Mean Doing Less

After he [Jesus] *had dismissed them, he went up on a mountainside by himself to pray* (Matt. 14:23).

Some of you may recognize the above passage of Scripture as coming from the chapter in which Jesus walks on the water. In this story, Jesus rescued Peter, who was being consumed by the waves.

Prior to this, Jesus had fed the 5000 by miraculously multiplying the five loaves and two fish and then spent intimate time praying to His Father. Jesus worked very hard, yes, but the results were often the result of time well-spent "refueling." Clearly, the value of solitude cannot be underestimated if we are to draw on the power of the Holy Spirit in our own lives.

Vince Lombardi, the championship coach of the Green Bay Packers, has been quoted as saying, "The only place success comes before work is in the dictionary." While there is unquestionable truth in the statement, coaches and athletes often take this to mean that one must be working *all the time,* because in the pursuit of excellence, there is no middle—either your performance is getting better or it's getting worse. The perfectionistic orientation associated with athletics generates a rather strange paradox: the work ethic is necessary, yet too much work creates problems. Where is the balance point?

The energy source for most athletic programs is the coach. You and I, as coaches, give the program life through our leadership and management of all aspects of the program, seeing to it that the program runs with effectiveness and efficiency. For this reason, we must also recognize that, like any machine, refueling is occasionally required.

Each of us needs to find those activities that allow us to totally disengage from the stress of the team. When coaching the team shifts from being fun to being a burden, that's a pretty good indication that your "expenses" are exceeding your "income." For full-time coaches, working a summer camp may take you out of the office, but you still stay linked to your job. Traveling to watch a summer camp session, even though you aren't working it, still engages your mind in the things of your job. Coaches need to allow themselves the freedom to "set aside business and go fishin'" and totally disengage from the mental, physical, and even spiritual rigors of the workplace.

Contrary to popular opinion, giving yourself some time to regroup, refocus, and recharge is entirely professional. The temptation is to listen to the critics who suggest that while you are relaxing somewhere, your competition is "out-hustling" you, therefore improving themselves at your expense during your leisure. What the critics fail to recognize is that rest is necessary, and indeed, biblical, for on the seventh day, even God rested! We must be ready to challenge the bogus drone of the critics who attempt to tell us we should be coaching 24 hours a day/seven days a week if we're professionals, or work at planning, strategizing, or coaching every evening and weekend if we're volunteers. The critics would have coaches be slaves, but guess what? We aren't serving the critics.

What we have is the freedom to choose our own definition and interpretation of success and the work ethic we use to arrive at it. If one of your athletes was pushing so hard as to approach burnout, how would you handle it? Would you tell them to press on anyway? Of course not. What advice would you then give yourself? It is virtually impossible to go beyond your limits indefinitely. If the time comes when just a little extra is necessary, you'll have nothing in reserve. One hundred percent is all any of us has to give, despite the many people who proclaim they are giving 110% or some such impossibility.

This season, give yourself permission to do the things you used to do before your coaching responsibilities became so demanding. Things like taking the family on a trip— without cell phones, fax machines, or e-mail—help keep life in perspective. Going on a canoe trip in the boundary waters of Minnesota or a river raft trip down the Colorado River, taking a camping trip in the mountains of Wyoming or just accompanying your kids fishing at someone's country pond can do wonders for your internal batteries. Maybe the best thing you could do is just stay home and perform some of the tasks your spouse has had listed for several months, tasks like repainting the guest bedroom, finishing the deck, shopping for some new clothes, or going go through those boxes in the basement. In any event, allow yourself sometime to get away, to do some of the things you like to do, along with some of those things you don't like doing. Giving something to yourself in this way enables you to maintain perspective on the issues that really matter. A fresh perspective brought back to your coaching may be just the advantage you can give to your team to add renewed energy.

Besides these trips or projects, remember that when Jesus stepped aside He spent time with His Father. When you become spiritually renewed, it will also affect your body and soul, and you will find yourself stronger because of it. Your inward investment in your relationship with Jesus will enhance your outlook...and your up-look.

"TIP-INS" FOR...Achieving More by Doing Less

1. Read, study, and pray. Quiet time with the Lord is never "down" time.
2. "Rest" is a "four-letter word," but how it's used determines whether or not it deters us from accomplishing goals. Jesus understood its value...so should we.
3. Never underestimate the value of authentic and humble prayer before God.
4. If you're working so much that it takes all your time and you never get a rest, then you're probably not working at the things the Lord would have you doing.

9

A Further Look at Motivation

But seek first his kingdom and his righteousness and all these things will be given to you as well (Matt. 6:33).

We often face some big challenges when it comes to consistently motivating our players to keep improving and to rise above the tempting illusion that success is a destination rather than a journey. We find ourselves investing in the activities that are the most *urgent* (like game films and practice plans) rather than those that are most *important* (relationships). Because motivation is often a very personal thing, it is understandably difficult for a coach to identify those "hot buttons" for each individual on the team.

In a fundamental sense, a motive is the desire to fulfill a need, but motives among players are varied and complex. Coaches are presented with issues of motivation in much the same way a conductor deals with the members of his orchestra. The conductor must find ways to bring out the best of each individual or grouping, combining talents and styles, blending the subtleties and nuances of each component to form a cohesive whole and bring beautiful music out of the instruments. To do this effectively, the conductor must be competent in his craft and knowledgeable about his/her group. As coaches, we need to be able to understand the parts we are trying to blend before we start building up the whole. In my own experience, motivating players individually can be one of the most delicate "dances" in all the relational dynamics of coaching—your partner can become a steady one who believes in you, or you can find yourself standing on the dance floor abandoned.

Coach Wooden told me of two simple motivational techniques he used for two guards that played for him. The technique for one was a pat on the back, the other he patted a little lower and a little harder! Indeed, both were different people and required different motivational tactics to fit each one's temperament. To treat them the same would have been unfair to both of them, and subsequently to the team.

Coach Wooden understood the big picture in Christ, and out of his concern for helping players reach their potential, he used techniques appropriate to each player, depending on the player's needs, not what was most convenient for the coach. Seeing himself as the teacher/catalyst, Coach Wooden moved to exercise his influence in order to achieve the shared goal of team excellence.

Roy Williams shared an experience with me in which he described an interaction with Michael Jordan while they both were at North Carolina when Roy was the assistant coach and Michael, the talented, but naïve freshman.

It seems that one day after practice as Michael walked off the floor, Coach Williams informed him he had had a bad practice. Michael's retort was that he had worked just as hard as everyone else. "Yes," Roy replied, "but you're not like everyone else—you've been blessed with more so you must give more." Michael had bought into the comparison "trap" and had been checking to see how he matched up with the others. But the coach knew if Michael was good enough to be better than his own teammates, then he needed to push harder than them to achieve excellence in his play. Michael hadn't understood real excellence at the time and was using the wrong standard.

Paul's challenge to the Galatians was interestingly similar to Coach Williams' challenge to young Michael Jordan. Paul wrote, "If anyone thinks he is something when he is nothing, he deceives himself. Each one should test his own actions. Then he can take pride in himself, without comparing himself to somebody else..." (Gal. 6:3-4). If we choose to be motivated by comparisons, we can always find someone better or worse than we are, and we will never get an accurate assessment of how we are truly performing. But if we set our performance up beside God's standard, then we will get an accurate assessment of both our failures and our victories, creating in us an internal motivational core with staying power. Our focus will become upward rather than side-to-side at our peers or downward toward those not as talented.

Team-oriented motivation often deals with the same kind of techniques as individual-oriented approaches. Some teams must be scolded, called to a higher level of performance because of principle rather than because of poor performance, perhaps saying: "That's not the way we do things here! First we will be best, then we will be first!" Other teams must be nurtured in much the same way as a parent puts his/her arm around a child as if to say: "I believe in you. Hang in there. I know you're struggling, but we'll get through." In each case, the bottom line is that the coach knows his/her team well enough to know when to scold and when to hold. Knowing that the coach is truly committed to seeing each athlete succeed is liberating and internally motivating because trust levels are reinforced and esteem is affirmed. Over time, the coach's message to his/her team becomes the difference between conditional and unconditional love. Players soon recognize whether they're either accepted at face value or they must meet the criteria before anyone approves of them.

Have you ever wondered how certain programs sustain the positive motivation to develop a winning tradition? It comes from elements that apply to both individuals as well as teams. The following principles of motivation instill confidence, enhance *esprit de corps,* and perpetuate intrinsic motivation, the fuel that fires the player's/team's inner drive to succeed.

Principles of Motivation

1. *Issue a challenge*—strive toward achievement and become passionate about one's purpose
2. *Share the dream*—the vision or goal; the "fuel for the "fire" that keeps bringing you back
3. *Give a sense of belonging*—being part of something bigger than yourself gives a sense of affirmation
4. *Participate in joint ownership*—be directly linked to the outcomes and activities of the group
5. *Enjoy the fun*—share satisfaction in a job well-done
6. *Apportion Success*—give recognition of progress

Motivation is not about manipulation or cajoling.

Rather, effective motivation calls upon an inner sense of purpose and passion for where we're going and how we're going to get there. There are no doubt countless extrinsic motivators, things outside our control that look good and do possess some level of satisfaction, but they don't last. As Christians, we are called to seek the kingdom first, and Jesus promises all these things will be given to us as well.

Here are some extended "TIP-INS" to enhance motivation levels in your program:

1. **Redefine success.** Jesus had the idea and its effects have remained unmatched. The purpose is to start measuring performance in terms of improvement vs. potential rather than in comparison to one's opponent, the scoreboard, coaches poll, or material gain. Through comparisons, it becomes easy to play at the level of your competition (the world) rather than to play to your own maximum potential (in Christ). If comparison playing is taught, in games against quality opponents, the team will be up; in games against lesser opponents, the team will be flat. *Winning* only happens to a few people some of the time while *success* can happen to everybody every day. With this in mind, losses are not failures; instead, they become feedback providing information essential to growth. When you redefine success, the standard of performance becomes something you can control rather than something you're forced to accept through following the standards of the media, colleagues, boosters, or even athletic administrators.

2. **Focus on the process rather than the product.** To consistently be victorious, one must first learn how to secure

the things from which victory is made. If one continues to improve and develop successful skills, concepts, and attitudes, at some point the outcome starts taking care of itself. Charting practice for hustle plays, taking charges, floor burns, and box-outs (for example, in basketball) reflect the importance of the little things which lead to big things. Knowing how to enhance the mental, physical, and spiritual strengths needed to win lays the foundation for consistent victory.

3. **Keep the faith.** Coaches and athletes can never give in to the temptation to lose hope that somehow one's laborious efforts are working to the betterment of self, teammates, and others, and preparing everyone for lives of productive service to families, occupations, and communities. According to Scripture, faith is "being sure of what we hope for and certain of things not seen" (Heb. 11:1). As coaches, we oftentimes can't see the fruits of our coaching until years later, when former players contact us. We may not immediately see the results of our labors, but we must have faith that somehow we are making a positive contribution toward the holistic development of others and believing in a higher purpose which we cannot see. Faith becomes the reassuring nudge to press on when it seems progress has stalled or when it appears there is nothing left to do. Success may really be in front of you, but you may not be seeing it.

4. **Persevere.** Hard work and preparation are essential ingredients to bolster confidence. "Stick-to-it-iveness" is born in a spirit of determination and dedication, bringing out the kind of confidence and motivation it takes to realize lasting success.

Vince Lombardi once said, "The more you invest in something, the harder it is to give up." Paul wrote, "For we are more than conquerors..." (Rom. 8:37) Such is the case in athletics as well as in life. Being dedicated to lasting excellence and determined to stay the course allows coaches and athletes to channel distractions and temptations through a filter called character. Perhaps the opportunity to go a different route is more alluring than achieving the ultimate goal, but the individual must eventually choose. Perseverance is at the heart of motivation, as it calls would-be champions to hold firm to the fundamentals and virtues that consistent and enduring excellence requires. As Phog Allen once said:

We should think of victory

only in that it gives us courage to face the

next battle. It is what the man thinks in his

heart that enables him to win.

—*Phog Allen*

SECTION III

MANAGING
THE PLAYERS

The focus of this section is to address
the "know-how" of coaching, offering several tools
for directly working with young players.

10

Shaping Positive Expectations

For in this hope we were saved. But hope that is seen is no hope at all. Who hopes for what he already has? But if we hope for what we do not yet have, we wait for it patiently (Rom. 8: 24-25).

All of us are capable of achieving more than we are currently achieving. Too frequently, expectations of others toward us or the expectations we set toward others are too low. Trying to satisfy the expectations of other people on some level becomes a little like chasing rabbits. People's ideas about what the coach or the team ought to be doing change direction like a rabbit running to avoid capture—either we can take to the chase, or we can choose not to engage and invest time in something more meaningful and ultimately, something of greater consequence.

The best place to begin examining your expectations is within yourself. Too often, we become more concerned with the expectations of others than with our own. Comparing our abilities to those of someone else weakens our mental fortitude. The mindset is one of insecurity in always trying to keep up or out-do someone else rather than setting your own standard. Expectations of yourself are the ones that matter the most. And as Christians, the expectations Jesus has for us as His children supercede everything. Beginning to shape positive expectations for others on an athletic team requires understanding what Jesus expects, and finding ways to satisfy His expectations as we work with our teams.

Let's begin by setting athletic goals in which the team can experience success every day, because that process builds confidence and momentum. Goals concerning the work ethic or enthusiasm are good starting ones. These become reference points that we can use to challenge players to work just a little bit harder than they did the day before.

Using short-term goals builds confidence by demonstrating smaller increments of progress. Young players need to see small successes often because their attention span many times doesn't allow them to keep working until the bigger success happens. As coaches, we can develop the understanding of delayed gratification by establishing a sense of confidence in the smaller steps, using essential building blocks like hustle, enthusiasm, camaraderie, or focus. Gradually setting their sights for long term goals teaches them hope, because we're expecting a positive outcome as a result of the team's diligence and commitment.

Think for a moment about when Jesus began to establish a positive expectation among the disciples and a process of transformation occurred. When a coach's servant-oriented and single-minded heart and hands begin to sculpt the players' attitudes and behaviors, a belief in how good the team will be starts to flourish. In time, the faith works to transform expectations and an excitement that comes with a real love for a great contest. No matter what happens the team will have found victory! Teams that know the real Spirit of a Champion, the indomitable Spirit of Jesus, will always stand with Him in the Winner's Circle, come what may.

To be sure, the essential ingredient in coaching is the individual relationship with each player throughout the season and, in many cases beyond, continuing to reinforce the things which were imparted throughout the year. In challenging the athletes to improve, always avoid humiliation and embarrassment. Find ways to instruct firmly, demanding maximum effort and focus with kindness and understanding, particularly when their teammates are watching. In the end, the athlete will become better at evaluating their own performance and more disciplined in focusing on their expectations rather than someone else's. As they understand that they aren't performing for you, but rather as a form of celebrating the athletic gifts God has bestowed on them, young athletes might begin to know that athleticism is a gift, and the only expectations that matter are those that God has for each of His children—ones that are positive and full of hope.

"TIP-INS" FOR...Shaping Positive Expectations
1. The key to helping others realize more of their potential begins with a trusting relationship; keep promises, be honest, and be committed to the long haul.
2. In Christ, there is no failure—only feedback. How can we not have hope and a positive expectation about the future?
3. Encourage young athletes to be positive, no matter

what. Use "put-ups" only—never "put-downs." Optimism must be the habit and the standard. In the words of Gen. Colin Powell, "Perpetual optimism is a force multiplier."

4. When the team begins to believe and trust in each other, they begin to believe in and pursue positive expectations.

11

Keeping Your Balance

What good will it be for a man if he gains the whole world, yet forfeits his soul? (Matt. 16:26)

In the clamor for first place, all of us can easily lose perspective about what really is important in life. The temptation is the logic that if we just win enough times, we'll somehow be satisfied and happy. We'll get all that we want in life, and in the end, we will be successful if only we can win. Our relationships will be better, our kids will be happier and healthier, money won't matter, and everyone will think we're cool, if we can just win and keep winning. Jesus had a different idea...

Balance is a fundamental, profoundly obvious, and essential principle in nature, and one that easily gets lost in its simplicity and commonness. The old school coaches used to say that if a player lost his balance, he'd be outplayed. It is a simple, fundamental concept: if the jump shooter is not properly balanced, chances are the shot will not be made; if the passer is not balanced, the passes will not be crisp or accurate; if a defender is caught on his/her heels or toes, the offensive player gains an advantage. Most coaches would also tend to agree that a team with balanced strengths of offense and defense affords the greatest likelihood of victory.

Fundamentals like these continue to be the essential building blocks for success. As coaches, we further want our athletes to be balanced in life as people—not just athletes—developing skills and attitudes that promote success and roundedness for the years when their playing days are long past.

Wait just a second. Doesn't that stuff sound like it came right out of the 1920s? It's older than Pop Warner and his pee-wee football program! How can balance and roundedness really be that important? Do you have to have character to compete well? Anyway, since kids are so athletic today, can't they practically make jump shots standing on their heads?

Today's world says that fundamentals and basics like balance don't really matter anymore. They further say that hard work, dedication, and commitment year-round to a sport is the only way a kid will "make it" because time away from sports developing "roundedness" only means that somewhere else an opponent is working to kick more goals, shoot more jumpers, lift more weights, run faster sprints, all with a single purpose, which is to win when battle commences on game night.

And let's not forget the coach. For the coach, balance only means time away from planning practice, reviewing practice, watching game film, scouting another team, visiting or phoning a recruit, answering letters, promoting the program, responding to parents' calls, and a host of other very important things. People associated with athletic teams really are busy!

Does any of this sound familiar? It seems like "the ol' soccer ball" isn't as round and balanced as it once might have been. Something clearly isn't right, and as Christian coaches, we really should know better.

What is implied above is that to achieve success in sports, certain sacrifices have to be made. Sacrifice is typically seen as noble and worthy of honor, which is often why throughout history, many sports figures have been recognized as models—they have made sacrifices others weren't willing to make. Still, wisdom must prevail for team leaders to be most effective.

Working hard, for example, is a classic value in sports, and indeed in life. Giving one's self to the cause of coaching does include a certain amount of sacrifice and dedication—after all, hard work, persistence, and self-discipline all require the ability to set other perhaps more enjoyable things aside to become single-minded and intently purposeful.

The perspective of this essential success value, however, must be kept in balance with questions such as, "When is enough indeed enough?" and "Am I working with equal focus in all aspects of my life?" Another challenging question is, "Is the Lord really at the center of what I'm doing?"

Balance in physical, mental, social, and spiritual aspects of life provides the foundation for continued growth, like a balanced diet. If I only ate cookies and pop for lunch, it might be fun and taste good, but my performance in the afternoon would be lackluster at best. At first, I'd be "wired" on sugar and caffeine only to then bottom out when the energy was burned off. Everyone needs balanced proportions of work and leisure, food and exercise, and socializing and solitude. Balancing academics and athletics is super, but there's more to life than just books and sports. As the age-old advice suggests, "Anything to excess is not good for you."

Thirty years ago, no one ever heard of a stress fracture or an overuse injury or "burnout." Today, coaches in virtually all sports have directly or indirectly experienced the pain of going too hard for too long. Sports pages today are replete with stories about ulcers, early retirement, stress disorders, and divorce because of the overwhelming demands placed on team leadership. Somehow, our society has bought into the thinking that winning is all that matters.

Clearly, setbacks and shortcomings are a part of life. Yet we often resolve them by creating a greater imbalance—to work harder, in greater detail, with keener focus, for longer hours until we've sacrificed ourselves right out of the reason we like to coach: because we enjoy it. Surely (we rationalize), as a result of our effort, then victory will come and we'll enjoy it more, right? Not always.

Perspective and balance are perhaps the two main ingredients that help us maintain equilibrium and direction in life and in sports. If sports are a place to learn about life and how to be more successful in it, what values must remain fully intact to enhance the learning of those balancing life lessons? The following are three of them.

Values That Produce Balance

1) **Unity.** Whether we want to admit it or not, we are all on the same team together, each assuming a role, and participating in the game of life. Because our ambitions of excellence often blind us to the needs of those around us,

we should be careful not to forget that we depend on each other to help us make the most of our opportunities. Individualism never has been part of truly successful athletics. Selfishness and petty differences only serve to divide programs and colleagues to the point where trust and teamwork no longer mean anything.

Indeed, families at home must also be nurtured in conjunction with the "family" at the gym or on the field if coaches are to enjoy stability and a comfortable environment away from the din and clamber of a competitive season. Most assuredly, a house against itself cannot stand. As parents and leaders, what will we model for kids? There remains no "I" in "TEAM;" and there is still great strength in numbers.

2) **Honesty.** Most coaches would agree that kids know when a coach tries to "put something over on them." As the old adage suggests, "There is no right way to do a wrong thing." Honesty and trust are the lubricants of relationships. Without these circulating within your team, progress is slow and unstable, attitudes will clash, and complaints grow louder. Media headlines today scream of ethical misconduct and violation, proclaiming that athletes and coaches are people who are clearly fanatics who can't seem to control themselves.

For all of us, the words of an American proverb bring to mind the importance of measuring ourselves, not in comparison to each other, but in relation to the higher ethics of Christendom, of which honesty is a part: "Don't measure your neighbor's honesty by your own." Honesty continues to remain the best policy and as with success, only *you* really know if you've done your best.

3) **Humility**. One of the quickest ways to induce psychological distress is to convince oneself that somebody owes us something because we are entitled. Humility, on the other hand, is the sense of putting the needs of others before our own. Humility is reflected in the tradition of cleaning up the locker room after a game or practice so that it looks better than when you found it. There is a sense of mutual respect extended towards the building custodian who may be of lesser title, but certainly not in importance to a successful program.

How many of us were inspired to get into coaching because of a coach we played for? Many great coaches have come from humble beginnings, always carrying with them the names of those individuals who helped them so they might achieve success. No one gets to where they are alone. Humility is often a physical manifestation of one's esteem toward other people. Because others have helped us, we have an obligation to help someone else, reinforcing a fundamental that coaches everywhere try to teach their players, that of the "assist."

These three enduring values continue to both challenge and inspire me daily. Some other coaching values that would certainly be worth noting are generosity—a willingness to share, sincerity—being genuine, decency—demonstrating kindness and good taste in behavior, industriousness—being diligent and skillful, resourcefulness—being adaptable and ingenious, cooperation—willfully working together toward a common purpose, and loyalty—faithfulness toward one's colleagues, commitments or duties.

Practical teaching in these areas may seem elusive, but consider the following suggestions and perhaps adapt them as needed for your team:

1. Arrange for your team to serve food to homeless people at the local shelters or to spend some time at the local retirement home. Give your players and coaches the opportunity to feel good about helping someone less fortunate get a hot meal or just some encouragement. Use this kind of teachable moment to stress the importance of humility and decency, and not expecting recognition in return, but rather feeling good about yourself in knowing you did something nice for someone else.

2. Take some or all of your players to church with you. Spiritual renewal—recognizing a higher purpose and a God bigger than you or I—is another way to give sports some perspective. What's more, kids may meet the right kind of friends in church rather than on the street or in the park. If church is too threatening, contact a youth group leader to address your team, focusing on the importance of spiritual issues and competitive pressures.

3. Challenge kids to be more than just players. After all, they represent themselves, their families, the team, your overall program, and the community. They have a responsibility not to let down those players who have gone before them and those who will come after. Explain why it takes a little more to be an athlete and someone who gets to wear your team's colors. Images are powerful—encourage your kids to be a positive image for those younger players who look up to them.

No doubt each of us has been involved with people that have placed an emphasis on balance and also had experience with those that did not. Where values are not in balance, individuals are disenchanted and frustrated with the daily grind of knowing something is amiss that they can't quite put a finger on.

Practice can then resemble a mental and moral demolition derby—the winner is the one who wreaks havoc with the rest of the group, all the while inflicting great damage on himself in the process. This success is short-lived because people of this mindset only live to do it all again tomorrow. Confidence grows, but in a negative manner, affirming in the performer that he/she really is not as valuable to the team as the others. Failure is haunting because one's weaknesses are exposed like a giant bulls-eye for competing teammates to shoot at, and there is no support, camaraderie, or *esprit de corps*. Balance in this scenario means knowing how to endure, walking the tightrope between confidence and despair. Fear, disguised as bravado, lurks every time the game or practice starts.

On the other hand, I have observed in those who lead balanced lives that they enjoy what they are doing and who they are doing it with, and as a result, everyone else involved is affirmed, challenging and pushing each other to improve. Generally, people realize more of their potential as people and as athletes and coaches because fear of failure and isolation are diminished. For these teams, winning is not the most important...but it still happens often, anyway.

There is a great paradox at work inherent in the kind of healthy balance I've just described. What may seem to get compromised in the short term is multiplied in the long term. The paradox is that by doing less activity in one area of life and involving ourselves in broader aspects of it, we can attain a greater satisfaction in what we do. There is a delicate and dynamic balance in doing the right amount of something that produces the greatest quality of result. We must remember that athletics, like life, is a great adventure. Because each day brings new and exciting twists for which we can never be fully ready, the best way to approach it is by being balanced because otherwise we'll be outplayed.

"TIP-INS" FOR...Keeping Your Balance

1. If all the "eggs" are in one basket (sports), what happens if the basket breaks?
2. Remind players to invest in the team by investing in the roundedness of themselves. Roundedness offers stability because a broader perspective of life has been engaged.
3. Avoid being "an inch deep and a mile wide." Build strength of character by engaging the mind and spirit along with the body.
4. On road trips, take in culturally interesting and meaningful sites.

12

Private Victories
Before Public Acclaim

Enter through the narrow gate. For wide is the gate and broad is the road that leads to destruction, and many enter through it. But small is the gate and narrow the road that leads to life, and only a few find it (Matt. 7:13-14).

And when you pray, you shall not be like the hypocrites. For they love to pray standing in the synagogues and on the corners of the street, that they may be seen by men. Assuredly, I say to you, they have their reward. But you, when you pray, go into your room, and when you have shut the door, pray to your Father in heaven; and your Father who sees in secret will reward you openly (Matt. 6:5-6).

The road to real and enduring excellence really is a road not often traveled, and I believe it's getting less traveled every year. Athletes and coaches seldom take themselves away from the action of the moment to examine themselves

71

as performers and as people. If we perceive the road to excellence as being the road of Christ, then each of us needs to look within—alone and away from the crowd and the team and the spotlight—to determine what path we are on. We need time alone with the Father, and once we rejoin the team, we will find we have taken a step or two further down the path to success.

Developing sport skills was once a bit like this inner examination: an on-going process requiring regular times of solitude and inner focus. At one time, it was not uncommon to find players practicing ball-handling skills alone, rebounding their own shots, grooving offensive moves against an imaginary opponent, creating and acting out game scenarios in their minds as they played them out on the driveway or at the park, all to hone their skills and competitive aspirations. Coaches sent a list of drills home with individual players and challenged each one to a singular responsibility—to conduct the workout such that no one would interrupt their focus; in essence, each was called to act alone—no cheers or applause, no high-fives from teammates—just quiet, focused practice. The drills were as much about character development and mental toughness as they were about training and developing skills. The desire to push one's character by pushing one's mental and physical resolve to improve was played out with no one to witness and understand the struggle, and the commitment, and the passion, except the performer...and the Father.

Training in solitude requires a uniquely greater mental fortitude than with the team; the battle against self is far more challenging than an opponent. Without someone nearby cheering, challenging, or cajoling, individuals can find a clearer focus, a self-determined satisfaction, a mindfulness of purpose in their activities as opposed to the relative ease of getting caught up in the hype of pick-up games. While competitive character may be revealed in public contests, it is nurtured privately through the carrying out of solitary, purposeful, and often tiresome tasks. Being obedient to the wishes of the coach can sometimes bring untold challenge...and untold rewards.

Looking at society in general, we see that solitude is not a popular option. Most people readily prefer being in a group. Trends in clothing, hairstyles, and attitudes among many groups seem to indicate that "whatever is good enough for someone else is good enough for me." The quick fix is the preferred path to success while persistence and self-discipline gives way to ease. Who is training the individuals that behave this way? Many young people apparently have not truly been trained to think and act for themselves, particularly about issues of personal discipline, work ethic, goals, and attitude. It is important to note that followership is not necessarily bad, but clearly, peer pressure can be.

Where groups often identify performance excellence by comparisons, the individual must learn to recognize performance excellence in goals and expectations privately defined. The struggle to make one's body, mind, and spirit conform to one's will is the personal struggle of champions. The subsequent effort to master one's abilities, without concern for what other people say or do, sets individuals apart. Commitment to and engagement in the on-going battle of personal mastery and self-discipline represents the heart of a champion, and in Christ, a battle already won.

Yet the inherent trap in comparisons to others is that

people evaluate their performance with something outside their control—someone else's performance. In the end, becoming your best is something personal whereas being first is something public, which means an individual may not be running in the same race with everyone else. Comparison is about ego aggrandizement and self-preservation whereas the individual quest for excellence in Christ is about personal satisfaction and vulnerability. Personal triumphs are mixed with the revelation of flaws and weaknesses. Jesus keeps coaching us upward.

"TIP-INS" FOR...Private Victories before Public Acclaim

1. Think of successes and failures as feedback, necessary information required to meet the next goal. Keep performance records and set personal goals based on immediately preceding performances. Perfect your game rather than working to perfect someone else's.
2. Challenge kids to be more self-disciplined. Self-discipline is nothing more than an on-going battle with one's human nature. Win one more battle than you lose each day. As the old coaching adage goes: Learn to discipline yourself so no one else has to.
3. Challenge kids to be wise, not just smart, and to make choices that are personally enhancing and socially redeeming rather than self-defeating. High expectations are necessary as most players will rise to the level at which they are expected to perform.
4. Reinforce an ordered perspective about sport and how it fits in life.
5. Recall that your God-given potential is totally unique and personal within you. Why compare yourself to someone else when you are not like anyone else?

13

Be More Demanding!

You were running a good race. Who cut in on you and kept you from obeying the truth? That kind of persuasion does not come from the one who calls you...(Gal. 5: 7-8).

Sometimes we're deceived into thinking that a life of ease would enable us to grow better. If we could just focus on the things that we like to do and are good at, we think we would truly do better at serving people around us. We'd feel good about ourselves because we'd be having fun. If only we wouldn't be distracted by the stress of life, we're sure that we could perform far better.

Funny how the cross-country race of life seldom offers a long down-hill stretch. The truth is that the authentic Christian lifestyle is extremely demanding, and young athletes must learn to relish the challenge of difficulty. As the old adage suggests: "Self-esteem and self-confidence don't come from being told how great you are—you get them by facing challenges and mastering them through hard work and persistence." And in Christ, we have the Coach right in the thick of life with us.

Most coaches and parents have done a great job encouraging kids to work hard at sports. Yet although lifting more weights, running more miles, and practicing more moves usually serve to make one a better player, each activity does not necessarily make one a better person. We can see the motor skills getting better, but it's much more difficult to see the character changes and the growth in the contents of the heart.

Being demanding of the athletic performance only gets part of the educational substance found in sports. If all the athlete has to focus on is his/her athletic contributions (even within a team context) during a season, they often miss the point about contributing in other ways toward other ends far beyond sport.

If we've been coaching for awhile, we know the contributions to a team are many and varied. Unfortunately, we can lose sight of the contributions of such things as who is offering the most enthusiasm or who is willing to carry the gear or who is willing to tell the better players to play harder. Each of these contributions offer some small boost forward, because it promotes kids who are willing to be selfless and are rarely being thanked or appreciated for their contribution. Indeed, sacrificing for someone else is easy when it's cheered and applauded. The challenge is often for young players to mature morally so that they can take the focus off themselves and put it onto ways to serve others, whether they don't play much or play every game.

Too often, coaches and parents remediate rather than accelerate expectations during the competitive season and the standard of excellence gets compromised. If kids are to learn how good they can really be, they need to be tested more during the season than in the off-season. The tests, however, need to be in areas other than academics and athletics because these are the ordinary rather than extra-ordinary measures of champions. Learning to establish a sense of priorities and goals are extremely valuable lessons, particularly as young players find that success in sports brings more and more distraction. Yet, because the athlete succeeds at things they are good at and comfortable with, it will require that we are more demanding of them to stretch and grow.

The tests I'm describing aren't designed to trip players up. To the contrary, the tests are designed to build them up, challenging them to grow in efficiency, maturity, focus, and patience, learning how to take first things first and deal with, for example, the business of homework before the pleasure of a ball game or practice.

Extra activities could include raking leaves or mowing lawn for a shut-in, or making a visit to a local retirement home or hospital. Activities could also include team duties such as sweeping the practice floor, getting the practice equipment ready, prepping the athletic training kit, or getting the towels from the laundry room. These aren't just the activities of managers, they are chores of the team and carry significant responsibility.

Just because an individual "suits up" for practice or games doesn't mean they are entitled to anything in a specific sense. These activities can become a scaffolding for team unity and serve to reinforce the principle of being responsible and accountable to others. Being more demanding isn't about making young athletes do busy work, but instead challenging them to take another step or two outside their comfort zone in the security of our presence and guidance.

"TIP-INS" FOR...Being More Demanding!

1. Remember that standards are set by the coach, not by popular vote of the team.
2. Teach persistence and perseverance—delayed gratification is the essence of why you practice.
3. Note that early success at small chores sets the stage for success at larger ones.
4. Learning to derive pleasure in service to the team allows a young person to be happy in any role, not just the starting one.
5. Be careful...coach in a manner that shapes their will without breaking their spirit.

14

Expect Less...
As a Challenge!

*Now fear the Lord and serve him with all faithfulness.
Throw away the gods your forefathers worshiped...and
serve the Lord. But if serving the Lord seems undesirable
to you, then choose for yourselves this day whom you will
serve....Then the people answered, "Far be it from us to
forsake the Lord to serve other gods!" (Jos. 24:14-16)*

The verse above gives us an example of sheer coaching
greatness. Joshua, the coach, puts the issue squarely on the
line. He wants to see what his team is really made of. He's
looking for a commitment to excellence, a commitment to
the Lord God of Israel. Joshua wants his team to stop set-
tling for second-place and put their trust in the Master of the
Universe. No longer can the team be complacent about who
they serve and how they are going to go forward. Joshua's
coaching makes it clear; either they're going forward as
champions in the Lord, or they will turn and serve another.

The principle of committing to excellence was something Jesus was intently passionate about, always coaching

people to strive for something better and to climb higher in the faith. Jesus constantly challenged those around him to consider their ways, set aside sinfulness, and begin to pursue the righteousness of God. His expectations were high; in fact, nothing less than perfection. Yet we know how easily we can get defeated, soon finding ourselves utterly imperfect beside the standard of the Lord. So, we back off, get lazy, and slowly begin to expect less and less of ourselves and those around us.

When we're serious about maturing in the faith and establishing intimacy with God, we feel challenged when someone, from a heart of honesty and love, informs us that they aren't seeing any signs of our growth or improvement. They perceive us to be less than we know we are and we're stimulated to action. In my own life, when a pastor or respected Christian brother or sister holds me accountable and reveals my spiritual foibles, it quickly gets my attention before God.

There is an expression in American culture that says people are a product of their expectations in life. Coaches know that this expression is profound in the development of athletes. Inasmuch as most of us have high expectations for the athletes as do the athletes themselves, plans for meeting those expectations are, in most cases, adhered to. Occasionally, however, we come across athletes who may not yet have developed the maturity, self-control, work ethic, and commitment to really go after goals with everything they have. In some instances, our expectations may be higher than what the athlete chooses to hold for themselves. How do we know? We go back to the preseason meeting when the athlete met with us and declared in very clear terms his/her expectations and plan of attack for the season. In our collaboration and support, the journey began with combining our direction and their response, the athlete rightly accepting responsibility for their own improvement. Over time, however, the athlete began displaying signals that they had gotten off track. Their performance deteriorated in the classroom, on the field or court, and in public, signalling the plan wasn't working. We began noticing an irritability and an ease with which inappropriate behaviors were engaged, and then dismissed, as if nothing had happened.

Here is where we as coaches, within the framework of being fair, consistent, and positive, can challenge the athlete regarding the breakdown. Keep in mind that it is the athlete who has the responsibility of choosing to meet the mutually agreed upon expectations. Therefore, you and I, as facilitator and evaluator of the team's well-being, must know if the given athlete is not able to meet the expectations, making it necessary for the coach to lower the bar.

In light of what has been consistently observed in the athlete's behavior, it becomes necessary to re-evaluate the initial plan concerning the athlete's development. It seems that either the bar was set too high by the coach, making it unfair to the athlete, or the athlete had an inflated view of their own abilities, or maybe the athlete has slacked off.

When the coach lowers the bar on a competitive person too soon, it represents an insult to the player's skills and abilities. Hallelujah! God, the Father never lowered the bar for Jesus, and He never lowers the bar for us. Instead, He calls us to perfection, not in our strength, but in His. He calls us to be champions, not by our talents, but by His sacrifice. Jesus never lowered the bar for anyone He met, and we can demonstrate to people that we won't either, pointing them toward Jesus, and gently revealing to others how inadequate each one of us truly is to achieve the goal of heaven.

Competitive people often respond favorably to a coach's challenge and honest assessment, as long as a trusting coach/player relationship is in place. The athlete may initially feel threatened and defensive, but as the player is honest with him/herself, and as maturity and the hunger for excellence kick in, their performance will begin to rise. If it remains sub-par and does not improve, the choices of the athlete become even easier for the coach to evaluate. As the coach presents an honest evaluation of the athlete's performance or behavior and finds it lacking, lowering the bar of expectation isn't a mind game, it is merely an attempt to place the bar where the athlete will have the greatest likelihood for success.

All of us can be challenged when we are made to realize that we are performing at levels below what we are capable of and what we know in our hearts we can do. Deceiving ourselves into thinking we're doing alright causes us to settle for something less than God's best. Jesus didn't settle for less than God's best, and neither should we.

"TIP-INS" FOR...Expecting Less...As a Challenge!
1. Consistent individual feedback allows players to know exactly where they stand in relation to a mutually established plan between player and coach.
2. The goal of Christ-like character is a "bar" set very high...but remember, we're not jumping in our own strength.
3. You don't have to be dramatic when you "put it on the line" with your players. A simple quiet conversation can communicate the expectation just as powerfully.

Section IV

Effective Relationships

The focus of this section is to highlight
the nature of positive and productive relationships
among players, parents, and coaches.

15

Communication

Preach the word; be prepared in season and out of season; correct, rebuke, encourage—with great patience and careful instruction (2 Tim. 4:2).

To be effective in our role as coach, we simply can't overlook one very important fundamental: we must be good communicators. Our model Coach—Jesus—gave us an excellent example of how to effectively communicate. Always mindful of the needs of the audience, He easily connected with all kinds of people using the appropriate words for each individual, spoken in the right way, and backed by His impeccable model of godliness. He always taught them in a language they could understand and never talked over their heads. Instead, Jesus spoke *to* people rather than *at* them. He made sure they understood His point, even if they didn't agree with it or felt threatened by it. After all, what good would it have done if Jesus, God incarnate, came to earth and communicated a message that no could understand?

Any kind of communication has three essential elements: a message, a sender, and a receiver. For effective communication to occur, the message must be sent and received without misunderstanding or misinterpretation. How easy it is to take this for granted when we communicate!

Miscommunication begins when senders and receivers consciously or unconsciously attach different values to the information contained in the message. If I haven't effectively communicated what "competitiveness" means and the value I place on it, how can I expect my athletes to simply figure it out on their own? The message of "competitiveness" contains both the meaning of my words as well as the meaning of my model. Communicating the right message is vital to producing the desired coaching effects.

For this reason, clear and effective communication must involve unambiguous delivery and receipt of information. In communication, listening is as vital a skill as speaking. Each of us actively listens by tuning in to words and voice tones while we may passively absorb gestures, facial expressions, and feeling the general tone of the interaction.

Effective communication also involves asking questions. For example, if you like fast food, you know the importance of a good listener asking the right questions at the drive-up window of a fast food restaurants to double check your order. Active listening is required to sort out the real core of the matter, the real subject that may be hidden by the words. The purpose is to check for understanding, to clarify what was heard, and to make sure the message is intact as it was originally intended. Efficient communication places a high value on clarification because, in many instances, the margin for error is very slim and misunderstandings can be costly. There also may only be time to send the message once.

For example, if we're playing in a close game and we're down to the final timeout, I may have only 60 seconds to communicate a plan of attack—not much time to repeat the instructions. As a coach, I must be prepared to keep my instruction clear and concise. Working with young athletes, it's difficult enough to communicate instructions without the pressure of the clock or the score, but when that's added in, we have a good test of our communication skills and so we learn...

When I challenge my players with an expression like, "What caused you to throw that pass?" I need to listen carefully to their response. If I expect an honest answer, something that I can use to help him improve, then I had better be prepared to truly listen to what my player saw, or thought he saw, that precipitated his action. If I don't understand his answer or want more clarification, I must ask a further question, just like peeling back the layers of an onion. Listening makes communication efficient and purposeful, and it enables us to more precisely target our coaching.

Application of these ideas can happen at home as well as in the office or on the court. Ultimately, the purpose in being precisely engaged in the communication process is to extend to the other party the notion that you care enough about them to understand them correctly and that you will take the time to do so. Subsequently, respect, trust, ownership, and accountability are nurtured in the individuals directly involved and in the team in turn.

Truly giving yourself to the act of listening to another is powerful. How many times have we been in someone's office having a meaningful conversation, when the phone rings, and we are the ones put "on hold"? The message that gets communicated is that the phone call is more important than we are. Intentional or not, if we're the ones answering the phone, we may be compromising our own value system in front of the very people we're trying to coach.

Always be ready to express the point of view of Scripture. Each of us has conversations everyday with our athletes, our families, and our friends about matters pertaining in some way to values or attitudes about life. Topics such as honesty, integrity, fairness, and trustworthiness are discussed all around us. If we personally are grounded in the Word of God, then we have an opportunity to communicate some level of moral authority to the conversation or activity, providing a perspective of truth, rather than wasting the opportunity with empty words. In communicating moral authority in your words and deeds, you are fulfilling the challenge of Francis of Assisi, "Preach Christ always—use words only when necessary."

"TIP-INS" FOR...Communication
1. Keep the message simple and in terms the receiver can understand.
2. Practice being concise, since most listeners will only retain about 30% of what you say.
3. Ask open-ended questions to draw out understandings in sensitive areas.
4. Asking, "What I heard you say was..." is an way excellent to "get on the same page."

16

Power Coaching

I pray that out of his glorious riches he may strengthen you with power through his Spirit in your inner being, so that Christ may dwell in your hearts through faith (Eph. 3:16-17).

Let's be clear...Jesus Christ is the power source for all believers. In Him alone, we have the power to do spiritual battle and win! And make no mistake, many of the issues that we are dealing with today have nothing to do with kids' talent levels or desire to be good athletes. Rather, the issues we confront are matters of the heart along with a spiritual emptiness in young people, if not blatant rebellion, caused by the deceptive influences of the enemy. As parents, as teachers and as coaches, we are clearly at war for the hearts and souls of our young people, and athletics offers a chance to make a difference. Athletics, for many, holds some glimmer of hope for a brighter future.

As Christians, we are to be humble servants before the Lord. Yet, having received the Spirit of Christ, we have tremendous power within us to do the work of the

Kingdom. How easily we are deceived when we don't grasp the strength of power the Holy Spirit provides in us! Whatever power we may exhibit, on our teams and in our homes, must be of God for it to accomplish His purposes. It's lost, however, if we aren't good stewards of the opportunities He gives us for His glory.

Power is the perceived ability of an individual to meet the needs of the group. As a result of meeting these needs, the leader receives loyalty, respect, and "followership." As one's track record of success in meeting needs grows, so does the perception of power in the followers. When big needs are met, great power is the perception. In most relationships such as player/coach, parent/child, boss/subordinate, trust becomes the central ingredient in generating power since real power is something earned, much like respect. In addition, as each of us can meet needs for others, so too is power available to everyone.

How do you go about obtaining power? One of the first issues to address must be motive. Are you motivated to meet Jesus in the stark and overwhelming realization of your own sinfulness? If a coach's perceived motive is selfishness, power will be recognized as a tool for the coach's betterment, not the team's. On the other hand, if a coach's motive is service, players and staff will be willing to subordinate themselves to the wishes of the coach for the perceived end result of success. The paradox seems to be that power is gained by giving up self-interest—our power grows when we stop concerning ourselves with ourselves.

Power can be manifested several ways, but the focus of enduring power must be on service to others. One way of generating power is giving yourself a timeout in the heat of battle. Removing yourself from the action allows you a chance to regain perspective about what you are trying to accomplish and evaluate your present course of action.

Jesus often went away to pray. He gained strength as he spent time alone with the Father, or in quiet conversation about the Scriptures with close friends, His disciples. Jesus knew the Source of Power and made conscious effort to connect with Him often.

A second way of generating power is to listen carefully to people around you. Some may be communicating verbally and others nonverbally. Powerful leaders are skilled at "listening" to actions as well as words. By asking people, "Is this what you mean?" we are extending respect and therein building trust. This process offers the leader a chance to get firsthand information about a person's needs and then a corresponding chance to meet them—a chance to exercise some power.

A third way of generating power is to disconnect from your own sense of status or rank and let people see who you truly are. When we attempt to exert power by "pushing" our agenda with the energy of our rank or title behind it, we alienate people. Try pulling a string across a table and it will go wherever you wish. Power, then, is being willing to give up perceived status and pull or attract people toward a goal rather than employing the often easier method of driving them with coercion.

"TIP-INS" FOR...Power Coaching
1. Follow the Golden Rule of doing to others what you would like done to you.
2. Practice balancing your perspective in the heat of battle by giving yourself a brief timeout.

3. Remember that listening extends respect and builds trust, two essentials of power.

4. Show the balance point of equal suffering—not equal job descriptions, but equal work—for each member of the team, including you. People accept a lot of discom-- fort when everyone is in it together.

5. Never allow yourself to gloat over the advancement of your own agenda. Save someone else's face as well as your own.

17

Be a Risk Taker!

Peter said to him, "We have left all we had to follow you!" "I tell you the truth," Jesus said to them, "no one who has left home or wife, or brothers or parents or children for the sake of the kingdom of God will fail to receive many times as much in this age and, in the age to come, eternal life" (Lk 18:28-29).

"Sometimes you have to go out on a limb...because that's where the fruit is." —Unknown

There are those defining moments of faith, just as there are defining moments in competition, that seem to secure an outcome in a given challenge. Call it "crunch time" or the "two-minute warning," the moment requires an intentional, and many times unrehearsed, act of courage and boldness to swing the pendulum of probability into our favor. When we find ourselves in this sort of "big dance," we'd better be past counting steps. At this point, we are being tested by a unique challenge that pushes us to the very limit of what we think we can do or bear. As we take stock of the situation as time permits, we either choose to embrace the risk and "go for it" without looking back, or we offer something less and later wonder whether our decision was right and whether our efforts would have been enough.

Several times during the course of games, we coaches are faced with situations that require an instinctive response—a calculated risk that distinctly shapes the course of the contest from that point forward. Veteran coaches draw on experience to help them decide the most effective course of action. Younger coaches are left to trial and error, but often draw on what they have seen veteran coaches do, having witnessed it at a clinic, through televised games, or by watching a practice.

It would seem that, over time, the "bench-coaching" component of a coach's duties becomes easier as each decision provides experience for the next, and the feeling of actual risk diminishes as confidence grows. Sometimes this observation is accurate, but many times not.

Still, many of us are finding ourselves in uncharted waters and overwhelmed, not as bench coaches offering in-game strategy or coaching, but as surrogate parents and models for our athletes. Many of our athletes have such a profound need for leadership and direction in their personal lives that we find our coaching tool box and emotional repertoire ill-equipped to meet the needs of the players for belonging, guidance, compassion, and love.

Some coaches may suggest that the fulfillment of these needs is not the role of the coach, but of the parents or other family members. This attitude is not too far removed from Charles Barkley's proclamation in a shoe commercial, "I am not a role model." There is usually a tendency to shy away from the risk of relationship when it may be "high maintenance" or when it might involve circumstances with which we, as coaches, are unfamiliar. Whether we desire to have the responsibility of meeting those personal needs of kids or not, we become, by virtue of our positions, a tangible symbol of hope, and can offer a relationship that often goes much deeper than just individuals sharing a common experience in sport.

What coach would not go to the hospital to visit one of his players if he/she had been accidentally hit by a car while riding a bike? This sense of obligation would no doubt be multiplied if the player was on his/her way to one of your practices. Clearly, our players become bonded to us in a unique relationship, just as we do to them. Whether we want to admit to truly caring for our players or not, crisis situations on a team can make things complicated for the team relationships. But why does it sometimes take a crisis before we let our players know we care? Wouldn't it be great if we didn't have to put on the bravado or the airs of the "coach" or athlete when we're with our teams? I think acting down-to-earth is good for players to see, because then they know we're for real.

The player-coach relationship is undeniably significant in the lives of athletes. It certainly has been for me. My dad was my first coach, and I suspect most of us got involved in sports because of relationships with parents, teachers, pastors, and coaches who wanted us to grow as people as well as athletes. Just as each of these coaches has touched our lives, we may feel compelled to touch the lives of others and make a difference for them as someone has done for us. Indeed, athletic coaching has the potential to be life-changing. But the coaching endeavor and its dynamic relationships are far from risk-free. Indeed, the player-coach relationships require a great deal of faith with planting seeds in them that we believe take root, even though we may never see the fruit until years later, if at all.

Relationships are seldom perfect and without complications or pain. The fruits of these coaching relationships, however, are often of such rewarding quality as to move coaches and athletes alike to smiles of affection or tears of joy. When the warm embrace of yesteryear is renewed at reunions, homecomings, or surprise visits to the gym or practice field, the bonds of love and common history quickly warm.

Indeed, the familiar sights, sounds, and smells of the old gym quicken the pulse and stir the memory, as you watch the old coach—your coach—take the team through practice one more time. The scene of young baseball players taking their places on the same field you did, brings you back to a time of innocence and possibility when your coach had you believing in yourself.

Now, as you watch those young kids, one of whom is yours, working hard, having fun, being challenged and chastised by the coach, it all makes sense. Yes…the lessons of life and of athletic excellence. The circle is complete. The feelings of love, affection, warmth, and compassion all serve to affirm both the coach and the athlete. The time spent together was good—not necessarily easy—but worthwhile and meaningful, and the rewards of the experience will never be measured by a scoreboard. Nope, just a smile, or a handshake, or even a hug from the old coach is all we need…and it communicates volumes.

Herein lies the greatest risk: why would we invest in

something so ambiguous as a coach/player relationship? Fortunately, somebody was willing to do this for us! Yet, even strong player-coach relationships are far from a guarantee of competitive victory every time we take the field.

We as teachers, coaches, and even parents must ask ourselves the real reason we have chosen to interact with young people. Building affirming relationships is risky business, but in the end, those relationships will be what endures far longer than the victories, trophies, and awards. The risk to follow the example of Jesus may not be as difficult as we think, if we put our trust in the Coach.

Sometimes, we do have to go out on a limb with people, but that's where we find life's sweetest fruits.

"TIP-INS" FOR...Being a Risk Taker!
1. Nurture your ability to coach from the heart by reading Jesus' coaching stories with His disciples. Become a good story-teller yourself.
2. Small relationship builders, like sending short, personal notes to your team, are small risks with huge payoff potential.
3. Be quick to listen, slow to speak when building relationships; we have two ears and one mouth for a reason...
4. Bring treats, like ice cream or Popsicles or candy, to practice, just to have some fun and let your kids know you were thinking of them.
5. Build good relationships with parents, too. The risk in getting to know mom and dad is minimized by inviting the parents to help you or the team in appropriate ways. Having a "mom squad" for pre- or post-game activities builds *esprit de corps* and trust.

Section V

The Mental Game

The focus of this section is to address the basic building blocks of mental excellence.

18

W.I.N. With Mental Toughness

Therefore, prepare your minds for action; be self-controlled; set your hope fully on the grace to be given you when Jesus Christ is revealed (1 Pet. 1:13).

The person telling you about the ball taking funny bounces is usually the person who dropped it.
—Lou Holtz

One thing I learned about sport psychology in graduate school is that mental toughness involves preparing for the contest ahead of time. Before the heat of battle commences, players and coaches are best served if they take time to mentally prepare for various adversities or challenges that could come up in the game and review unique elements of the arena or field in which they will soon be playing.

One example is the case of playing a football game at the University of Nebraska. When unprepared players walk into that kind of setting on game day without mentally preparing for the sea of red, the pep band, and the tradition, they can quickly become disoriented (to the delight of the Nebraska partisan faithful).

Peter gives us the same kind of encouragement for our faith as a coach, working to enhance the team's mental edge before the big game. Make no mistake, our spiritual enemy is deceptive beyond our knowing, yet we can anticipate the distractions that come when we are on the offensive and Jesus' grace is being revealed in our lives. Our minds, as well as our hearts, must be strengthened and prepared by a steady diet of prayer, fasting, and study in the Word.

Mental toughness, it seems, is one of the most difficult skills for many athletes and coaches to acquire. Mental toughness is a composite of attributes that allows performers to stay focused under pressure and to thrive in the heat of battle. Yet distractions are such an intrusive part of sports that it is often difficult to hold off the noise and be focused on the task at hand, staying in the "now" moment instead of in the past or the future.

So how can we best begin to claim mental toughness as one of the tools with which we "do battle"? Initially, performers must recognize that mental toughness is a learned skill; and like most learning, it requires a fair amount of practice to make it consistently strong. The development of mental toughness is a process, and like virtually all processes it has a starting point. The starting point involves two components: awareness and perspective.

The *awareness* component initiates the process of getting mentally tougher. We have to first become aware of our present state of thought in order to change or go another direction. It stands to reason that we must be aware of where we are before we can begin to change, modify, or adjust.

For instance, ask your athletes for their exact thoughts during a moment in practice, just after you have stopped the action. See if they can respond and then ask them to determine if those thoughts were performance-enhancing or performance-defeating. You'll be surprised at the lack of attention athletes give to their own thoughts about various situations, particularly challenging ones. The strategy here isn't to foul up the links between mind and body by making them think about their own thoughts just as they need to make a play. Instead, it is to help them become aware of what they think, when they think it, and how they can think better, particularly under pressure conditions. Developing a mental game plan for challenging moments helps.

The second component of the process is *perspective*: being able to recognize important cues in a given moment, particularly the cues that will lead to an increased likelihood of success. Once an appropriate mental perspective is established, which places the mindset in the present time and exact moment, young athletes can allow previously trained skills and tactics to function without being unnecessarily jumbled by distractions. At this point, performers have made specific effort to focus on outcomes they want to happen, rather than leaving them to chance.

One of the best mental cues I've found for this initial phase of mental toughness development is a tool I picked up from the coaching "tool box" of Lou Holtz, football coach at the University of South Carolina. In three simple words, Coach Holtz crystallized a powerful reminder representing both components of awareness and perspective. His phrase was "What's Important Now" –W.I.N.

This particular tool could become an individual or team rallying cry when faced with pressure-packed moments of competition. It offers the performer a mental signal to become aware by mentally checking in to the important situational factors and secure a perspective for the immediate moment.

Phrases like this allow young performers to mentally take control of a challenging situation by providing a mental cue directed toward excellence rather than directed away from failure. Through it, they are able to sort out all the complex strategies, emotions, and thoughts that go with athletic contest and condense it all down into a moment-by-moment, one-step-at-a-time advance through the game.

"TIP-INS" FOR...Mental Toughness

1. Be sensitive to the ability of kids' minds to start running too fast under intense game conditions. Just because the game is running fast doesn't mean your mind does, too.
2. Use words like poise, patience, perseverance, and preparation in teaching young athletes a resilient mindset for competition—one that can bounce back effectively.
3. Mental Toughness is always enhanced in an atmosphere of trust and camaraderie.
4. Reducing mental thoughts down to two or three confidence-enhancing key words or phrases allows the mind and body to sync up much easier under pressure.
5. Failing to prepare is preparing to fail.

19

Perform Consistently in Chaos

The end of all things is near. Therefore be clear-minded and self-controlled so that you can pray (1 Pet. 4:7).

Being clear-minded and self-controlled is often the difference, in athletics and in life, between victory and defeat in the midst of uncertainties. The ability to see clearly the goal we are pursuing, while demonstrating the self-control and poise to achieve it, allows us the opportunity to perform consistently in the midst of chaos. Jesus lived this principle and Peter understood it well, writing to all believers as an encouragement and as an antidote to confusion and anxiety.

There is no question that sports is one of the most dynamic endeavors ever pursued: players are continually moving; offensive and defensive strategies shift and adjust; the ebb and flow of transitions from offense to defense never happen in exactly the same way. Yet, most coaches would agree that there are a variety of patterns that tend to emerge in various situations, a sort of "if they do this, then we do that" scenario. While coaches can readily see these patterns, their dynamic nature is often difficult for players to deal with and consequently, the resulting confusion on the floor results in poor performance. Could there be a way for coaches to teach players a consistent set of thoughts and behaviors that could enable them to be successful under any circumstance?

Earl Woods, father of golf phenomenon Tiger Woods, brought an intriguing strategy to the problems associated with the ever-changing dynamics in golf. Because of his military training as a Green Beret, Earl Woods had learned the value of what the military had termed "Standard Operating Procedure" (SOP) (Woods, 1997). This kind of approach would help Tiger routinize each aspect of his shot-making customs regardless of the kind of shot he had or the conditions surrounding it. While golf is radically different from team sports in its nature, the quality of highly disciplined focus under competitive duress in each sport is essentially the same, each calling for structure, precision, and purpose in mental approach.

Pete Carril, former Princeton coach, had a similar strategy for addressing the dynamic nature of basketball, which helped his players develop a singular focus and purpose in what they were doing. In *The Smart Take From the Strong* (Carril, 1997), Coach Carril described the importance of a "modus operandi" (MO), the consistent, standardized, habitual approach to performance. Carril said:

> I tell my guys that if they work hard every day, then they don't have to worry about game plans, or where they play, or whom they play, or about rankings and so on. The quality of their work habits can overcome anything: praise, criticism, good or bad coaching. I

try to get them to understand: if they learn to do things right, or well, that gets to be the way they do things, and whatever happens, that isn't going to change (p. 36).

The whole idea behind each of the two concepts explained above is that they allow a team or individual to direct effort and attention in a purposeful and effective way under any conditions. Where some coaches might prefer each athlete to have the same SOP, other coaches might allow individual athletes to identify their own SOP (in collaboration with the coach), personalized to them, and something in which they take ownership. Where the modus operandi becomes a standard for performance, the SOP is the logical and sequential progression of thoughts and movements leading to an effective outcome.

Typically, an SOP involves observation of the situation, followed by a selection of a strategy, and concludes with a specific action cue. Additionally, the effectiveness of an SOP initially relies on the coach's ability to teach fundamentals and to identify specific cues for the athletes to observe and recognize. Once this takes place, the player can become responsible for many of their decisions during the game without always having a coach tell them what to do or where to go. These decisions get condensed into short, specific cue words or thoughts that trigger focus and movement.

Could a modus operandi and SOP be useful to individual players as well as a team? In the case of individual application, a modus operandi like "work hard" is easily grasped and will indeed have far reaching effects after the athlete's game playing days are over. The SOP may likely be a bit more personalized, since individuals possess different strengths and attributes to draw on in competition. For example, "play smart, play hard, play fair" could be effective for one player whereas another player may have an SOP like "Analyze-Anticipate-Attack." Naturally, whatever SOP an individual implements, it must be consistent with the goals and objectives of the team, and something that can be carried from game to game.

One might recognize that the modus operandi is an umbrella under which the SOP fits. The modus operandi is the guideline while the SOP is the set of steps to function within the guideline. While "Work Hard" is a modus operandi, "Ready-Respond-Refocus" could be standard operating procedure for many teams. In both cases, a large set of teachings about how you, as a coach, want your team to perform are condensed into specific, concrete performance checkpoints that you believe will lead to success. However, these performance checkpoints only take on significant meaning to your athletes if they are continually taught and reinforced daily in practice.

The age level that you coach may have some impact as to the meaning you give a MO or an SOP, affording players the opportunity to grasp complex ideas in a simple way and assert this knowledge under game conditions. Ideally, a coach tries to educate players so that they *respond,* rather than *react,* in competition. The learning process that enables this to occur takes time, patience, and dedicated effort before it becomes second nature to the player. However, the benefit of this approach is that players are better able to precisely focus on important information cues rather than becoming distracted by the officials, the crowd, the "big play," the trash talk, or all the psyche-out activity that doesn't really matter.

References:
Carril, P., & White, D. (1997). *The Smart Take From the Strong.* NY: Simon & Schuster.
Woods, E., & McDaniel P. (1997). *Training A Tiger.* NY: Harper Collins Pub.

"TIP-INS" FOR...Performing Consistently in Chaos
1. A "bedrock" mental, physical, and spiritual approach for competition eliminates guesswork. "Staying the course" will, given time, produce success.
2. In the throes of great adversity, take heart! Jesus has overcome the world!
3. Being intentional about how pre-game time is spent helps enhance a sense of confidence. Consistency in preparation translates into consistent performance, because the approach to chaos has been established in practice.
4. For the believer in Christ, there is no failure...only feedback.
5. Simulate chaos events in practice so young kids learn to respond to them. The events don't have to be probable to be effective. The challenge for the kids is to keep the focus and stay in the now.
6. Always debrief chaotic conditions after games or practice to maximize the learning in the "teachable moment."

20

Patience Enhances Consistency

Not only so, but we also rejoice in our sufferings, be-cause we know that suffering produces perseverance; perseverance, character; and character, hope (Rom. 5:3-4).

Sometimes the hardest thing to do in the Christian walk is to be patient. When things are going well, we want to go faster, farther, and better—we are impatient. And especially in the midst of struggle or suffering, God, it seems, can never move fast enough to get us out of the problem. Even after we remember that He is God, we still seem to grow impatient more easily than we might like.

Coach Paul knew a few things about patience, suffering, perseverance, and indeed hope in Jesus. Where we often see adversity as a sign of trouble, Paul sees opportunity. Paul realized that struggling was a sign of growth, that adversity meant not that he was being punished by God, but rather was being perfected by Him! Indeed, Paul's challenge to the Romans is also a challenge to us—when we see the value of a situation that requires us to be patient, God is growing us toward something bigger for His glory.

In a conversation I had with former University of Nebraska head football coach, Tom Osborne, he made a simple statement that I believe has profound importance for coaches and athletes in all sports. When asked about how long it took to win his first National Championship at Nebraska, he simply and matter-of-factly said, "

Success Takes Time.

—Tom Osborne

Osborne had been coaching football for over 30 years! Simple wisdom with profound meaning.

Sure, great teams are composed of great players and coaches. Sure, scheduling is a factor. Sure, winning makes it easier to recruit. And yet, when players and coaches seriously consider the nature of the games they love, the difference between excellence and mediocrity boils down to consistency and commitment, usually over extended periods of time.

Many coaches get jumpy when the scoreboard occasionally reflects disfavor towards their teams. The tendency in preparing their teams shifts from "staying the course" to quickly setting a new one. New plays lead to new formations, which lead to new strategies and new personnel modifications. Modifications must assuredly be made when players get injured or when academic problems arise, or even during the course of a game as tendencies and patterns emerge. Even so, a great deal of security for both players and coaches is rooted in knowing that an established mission is firmly in place.

From the beginning of the season we have been training all of our players to function within certain understandings about the strengths of the team, the style of play for the team, and the corresponding roles for each team member. In addition, we have demonstrated and preached values and attitudes we want our teams to grasp and apply. However, regardless of how good the team is, the level of performance many times stall out, even if only for a short time, before it continues upward. When the performance of the team sputters, it is likely that the previous understandings about the team and its values and attitudes remain true. The problem may only require a slightly different training approach from the coach to get things rolling again.

To the extent that our team is undergoing a trial, character is being molded and hope is being refined. What may need to be adjusted isn't the players' approach to competition, it is the coach's approach to the players. Maybe the last thing the team needs at this particular time is for the coaches to start pressing, trying to force the action or accelerate the learning curve before the team is ready. "Staying the course" provides a certain psychological stability and tempo necessary in battling tough challenges. The consistency mindset becomes the very foundation, established by the coaches early in the season, that enables athletes to endure a season with many peaks and valleys. The consistent mental toughness called on in the toughest times of competition is the fortitude borne of confidence and a belief in personal preparation, forged in numerous battles and contests.

What kind of message does a coach send when, under a particularly stressful period of the season, adjustments of varying complexity are made in practice almost daily? New offenses are installed, new personnel are mixed in, new defensive schemes are employed continuously. Does this promote confidence in search of answers or does it promote anxiety and the fear of losing another game? Naturally, the pursuit of excellence requires that individuals continue to seek new paths and new ways in which to conduct the pursuit. But that pursuit doesn't necessarily mean that a coach should make a change simply for the sake of change or for lack of a systematic approach to troubleshooting the team's performance.

The consistent coaching excellence of perennial champions does not often come quickly. As coaches constantly continue to learn from each season, it is only logical that, at some point, for a combination of reasons, coaches find what works for them. Much like Coach Wooden has said, "Many coaches get so busy learning the tricks of the trade that they never learn the trade." To learn the trade of successful coaching well and develop it to its highest levels, undoubtedly takes time.

"TIP-INS" FOR...Staying Patient
1. Many of God's most influential promises are those for people undergoing trial or who are suffering. Take God at His Word... and take hope.
2. A patient mindset facilitates poise. Trying to force the action is never a good replacement for making the most of the opportunities in a game.
3. Ask yourself if God is patient with you. Doesn't it follow

to be patient with others and allow His timing to work and perfect the situation?

4. Find God's flow and rhythm, and serve him by helping others find it too.

5. Remember, hope is a "future-oriented" word. Stay patient by grasping hope, because with hope in Jesus, there is more future than you or I can imagine!

21

Five Keys to Overcoming Adversity

...for everyone born of God overcomes the world. This is the victory that has overcome the world, even our faith. Who is it that overcomes the world? Only he who believes that Jesus is the Son of God (1 John 5:4-5).

Life is 10% what happens to me and 90% how I react to it. —*Chuck Swindoll*

The early church must have been a really special group of people. Think for a moment about the challenges they were up against and the message they would carry forward about a crucified man resurrected from the dead. Sounds more like a fairy tale, doesn't it? The culture was contaminated with many different kinds of ungodliness and immoral behavior, and it was up to the growing army of Christians to take up spiritual arms and do battle. Do you think there was any adversity?

There is no athletic season or competition without some form of adversity. The adversity presents itself often as injuries and occasionally as a case of bad attitudes, or even player suspensions. What separates the great teams from the ones who never recover is not found in the quantity or severity of problems a team faces but in how they respond to them. The championship teams find ways to thrive in spite of the problems. The expression, "A hammer shatters glass... but forges steel" is the battle cry of those performers who refuse to succumb to the illusions of fear and the paralysis of uncertainty.

What illusions? How about the one which suggests that due to an injury, your team no longer can win? Or the one an overly critical media would have coaches believe—that even though we have outstanding seasons, we must "win the big one" to be deemed great. Or the fearful discomfort associated with parents who become divisive after a loss. And, lest we forget, the one which implies that unless the coach wins, the coach is not competent. These are just a few of the faulty assumptions many coaches, players, fans, and administrators make when the veil of adversity descends on a program.

In some instances, adversity disappears by itself without a concerted effort to deal with it. Time is the key factor and, in the end, the adversity becomes muted and less severe as time advances—time *can* heal wounds. In most cases, however, programs are not in the position of having the luxury that allows time to take its course—the adversity must be addressed proactively and in a timely fashion.

Strategies for handling adversity:

1) *See the adverse circumstances as a challenge* rather than a

threat. Competitive people respond to challenges rather than react to threats. Is the situation managing you or are you managing the situation?

2) *Envision the lofty ultimate goal.* Developing a clear mental picture of the "best-case scenario" outcome puts your mind in a positive set and alerts your spiritual and physical resources to purposeful action.

3) *Focus on a daily goal plan.* Be sure that positive momentum is established with daily successes before the long-term plans are launched. Be results-oriented while process-focused—keep a future-oriented perspective while deliberately and purposefully acting in the present.

4) *When frustration sets in, take time to look back at your progress.* Oftentimes, looking back is a positive activity because it helps you maintain perspective. Taking a break from the action isn't necessarily a bad thing. If a lantern isn't properly refueled, the light it produces for others isn't going to be very bright.

5) *Remind yourself that the value of the success is measured in the volume of sweat.* Those things in which we place great value are generally those things for which we have worked the hardest to achieve. The more difficult and grueling the struggle, the greater the sense of satisfaction and pleasure when victory is realized.

"TIP-INS" FOR...Overcoming Adversity

1. Without pressure, a piece of coal never transforms into one of the most valuable and hard substances known to man: diamond.

2. Surrendering to the sovereignty of Christ is the beginning of peace in the midst of trial. See Phil. 4:6-7 for awesome encouragement in adversity.

3. Read the Bible to find God's road map for the way out of the crisis.

4. God's answers to our questions are often simply, "Trust and obey."

5. Battling through tough times is hard work. Put on the "full armor" and take time to mentally, physically, and spiritually rest.

22

Sharing Talents
for Team Achievement

All the believers were one in heart and mind. No one claimed that any of his possessions was his own, but they shared everything they had (Acts 4:32).

Take a moment to reread the Scripture above and consider it from the standpoint of an athletic team. Think about the sense of camaraderie and connectedness on the team— one heartbeat, one soul, one focus, one purpose, and one mission.

On the other hand, there is no question that an essential element of high achievers is the element of competitiveness. Competitiveness should not be so much against another person or team as much as it should be against one's potential. In Scripture, Jesus coaches us to compete against our own human nature—those things of the flesh that would lead us astray and deter us from victory. But how do successful coaches create that kind of competitive atmosphere in their programs that builds and inspires top performance, yet still facilitates love, respect, and shared purpose?

Because most players thrive on competition, many of the practice drills and activities determine a "winner" and a "loser." The key ingredient in making this approach build team morale is understanding that while a winner and loser will be determined, individuals are pushing each other to get more out of *everyone's* abilities, thereby benefiting the team. The mindset isn't "me vs. you" but rather "I push you, and you push me."

The result is a win/win that occurs between teammates who are more interested in giving effort to build the team or a teammate than they are in receiving a reward. Interestingly, this attitude goes against human nature, since most people want to know "What's in it for me?" Therefore this attitude must be taught (or caught through coach's example) before it will become a habit. The purpose is to use competition as a tool for learning and a checkpoint for progress rather than victory or defeat being an end in itself.

For example, in building a youth basketball team, in the first year of play the team may win only one or two games. But if the team can begin to understand that the coach is teaching them skills not just for this season but for the coming years, they can settle down to work on their skills and come back the next season with something the coach can build upon.

An essential understanding must exist that competition is only a tool that brings out a person's best. The goal remains victory. However, if competition means a threat to identity, playing time, or status, then the meaning of competition becomes more like "win-at-all-cost" to protect oneself. Playing from a defensive mindset is not the mindset of champions. A mindset that is on the offensive, playing to win, is always preferable to a mindset of fear, playing not to lose. As we push each other—me against you, you against me—we are surely competing, but cooperating in that we both want to help each other get better for the good of the team and the advancement of the team's cause. For believers, our offensive mindset is about advancing the Gospel, not necessarily about showcasing our talents. And yes, it does matter if we win or lose in the advancement of the Gospel.

As players learn to discipline themselves in this way of thinking about competition, each practice becomes a new opportunity to go farther than the practice before. Each game, no matter who the opponent, becomes an exciting discovery—to see how good we can really play, instead of "playing up" to the level of good teams and "playing down" to the poor ones. The players become internally motivated as they challenge themselves against themselves rather than against something or someone external. If the team, as a group, adopts this mindset, the challenge of games doesn't rest in the opponent, it rests in the team itself. Each game becomes a new adventure, full of discovery; and each practice becomes a purposeful and binding crucible of positive energy as teammates push each other to new heights.

"TIP-INS" FOR...Sharing Talents for Team Achievement
1. Use competition to foster cooperation by focusing on assisting a teammate rather than getting a reward oneself.
2. Stress competitiveness against self. Opponents, rankings, and rewards are out of one's sphere of control. Control of self is the greatest challenge.

3. Always look for improvements rather than mistakes.
    Mistakes are only feedback on areas where improvement
    is needed. Competition brings these things out.
4. Our gifts and talents are not ours. For the good of the
    team, we must share what belongs to God, so that all
    the believers might become better—some might be
    pushed; others might be lifted.

23

Directing Attention

Let your eyes look straight ahead, fix your gaze directly before you. Make level paths for your feet and take only ways that are firm (Prov. 4:25-26).

"If God wanted us to be focused on the past, we'd have eyes in the back of our heads." —Lou Holtz

When you think about it, the expression "the pursuit of excellence" implies that excellence is in front of us so that we might pursue it. In the same way, Jesus has a hope for us now and in the future—one that includes an eternity with Him in heaven.

Part of the beauty of coaching and athletic endeavor is that each day represents another opportunity to improve in some dimension of God-given abilities. This, of course, isn't just true of athletics; it's true in life. The unusual thing about athletics, however, is that the improvement process is witnessed by many people, and the performers are open to direct and immediate scrutiny of their performance.

Many times, the pressures of this kind of evaluation cause performers to become conservative and to focus on

120

avoiding defeat rather than on pursuing victory. Because athletic performance is a public experience, performers naturally are interested in protecting their identity, their privacy, their sense of esteem, and insulating themselves from their critics. Combatting this mindset, Coach Wooden has said:

Never listen to too much criticism—

it will affect your coaching;

never listen to too much praise—

it will affect your coaching.

—Coach Wooden

The challenge to pursue competitive excellence is a potentially risky undertaking because there are no guarantees of success and one's performance will be critiqued whether the effort ends in victory or defeat. What's more, the results of the contests and their subsequent public critique may become irrationally linked to the way we think and feel about ourselves. The "fiery arrows of the evil one" (Eph. 6:16) begin to chip away at our sense of whom we belong to.

As competitive seasons progress, coaches develop a good understanding of their team's weaknesses and strengths. In most instances, we have experienced some setbacks in the form of losses, injuries, academic problems, and a host of inter-team scenarios that could set the stage for the potential devastation of a season's worth of growth and improvement. The team's critics and supporters alike are all interested to see how the team is going to finish out the season—will they choke or will they be tentative? Will they find ways to snatch defeat from the jaws of victory? Will they play to win or will they play not to lose?

One fundamental principle to effectively deal with these complex questions is to not allow the group to get caught in, as Stephen Covey describes, "the thick of thin things." All of the distractions, ranging from elements of past performances to future expectations, can be set aside by embracing an aggressive mindset of playing to win versus playing not to lose. The challenge is to perform in the present—to "see" the target as being within reach and to unabashedly pursue it, playing with enthusiasm and hope. In spite of the score, the circumstances surrounding the team, the rankings and win/loss records, the group can find refreshed focus from within.

How does the coach communicate this to the players? One of the most important actions a coach can take is to remind the players again and again of his/her commitment to team goals that focus on fundamentals and then push the players to do what they do a little better and a little longer during the course of a game. State the goals in clear behavioral terms.

Another thing coaches can do is to encourage the players to "be thermostats rather than thermometers," i.e., placing attention on making things happen rather than watching things happen or reacting to them. Reinforce that athletics are meant to be played with emotion, passion, and enthusiasm, and that they should use that energy toward the good of teammates. Make the other team react to you.

We must also promote "calculated risk-taking"—the realization that oftentimes a team has to go out on a limb because that's where the fruit is. The team has to be willing to "take its foot off first in order to head toward second." In committing to this type of mental approach, the adverse distractions are set aside by default—one's mind cannot be in two places at the same time; at once in the past or future and at the same time in the present. Risk-taking can be loads of fun, particularly when you're doing it with friends, and if players aren't afraid of a coach ripping their heads off because they missed a play.

In the end, anyone who sets out to do something others have not done or are not willing to do, sets themselves up for criticism. This is, in a sense, an aspect of leadership—the idea that when a person makes a conscious decision and concerted effort to get ahead of the field, there will be distractions and criticisms trying to hold them back. If leadership is largely about one's example, we, as coaches, have a great opportunity to model for our teams the way to boldly pursue goals by playing to win rather than not to lose, and to direct attention toward things of value and lasting significance.

"TIP-INS" FOR...Directing Attention

1. You don't have to worry about poking your eyes with your hair brush as you brush the back of your head. There's a good reason why your eyes are where they are.
2. Select simple "targets" to set your sights on: things like your own enthusiasm level or the language you use to encourage or teach. Little things turn out to produce big results.
3. Sort distraction from things of importance by mentally rehearsing your game plan ahead of time.
4. Use a mental checklist to zero in the right thoughts, just as NASA has a pre-flight countdown. With practice, young athletes can learn to separate the "wheat" from the "chaff" in the competitive arena.

Section VI

The Team

The focus of this section is to illustrate the vital importance of a team concept among young players, parents, and coaches.

24

How to Build Shared Ownership in the Team

The body is a unit, though it is made up of many parts;
and though all its parts are many, they form one body.
So it is with Christ. For we are all baptized by one
Spirit into one body—whether Jews or Greeks, slave or
free—and we were all given the one Spirit to drink
(1 Cor. 12:12-13).

Shared ownership in the workings of a group of people is a "classic" Christian model for the workings of teams, families, organizations, and nations. To be sure, members of any group bring different strengths and abilities to contribute to the welfare of the whole, yet something typically keeps them from sharing, from giving all that they have, and trusting that they will receive all the others have. We resist making ourselves vulnerable to others and susceptible to their goofs that may have an impact on us. So instead, we commit just enough to contribute, but in the end, we still look out for ourselves and end up holding something back. Not giving one's all stems from a lack of trust, both in others and in Jesus. Yet our commitment and sacrifice for others is the ideal, it's the way of Jesus, and it's humility personified.

Learning to work together within a team is absolutely one of the most important lessons I learned as a young athlete. My Dad had my brother and I fielding ground balls in the backyard, always encouraging one of us to back the other up, which is to get behind the fielder in case the ball might squirt past him. This elementary model (two people working together to field ground balls) set the stage for working within groups of a larger scale. The size of the group changes, but the principle remains the same.

The concept of a team, as Paul states in his letter to the Corinthians, is one of the most powerful lessons any young athlete can learn through our athletic practices and games. While each player may have different talents or roles, each is vital in full contribution to good of the whole.

Every individual on the team has a task to perform before the team will realize its greatest potential. As people contribute their abilities to the cause, each becomes a vested partner in moving the team closer to its goals. Getting individuals to accept their role as part owner of the team is many times challenging for both the coach and the athlete. Strength of relationship between player and coach must be secure before there's enough trust to foster connectedness among the whole.

Coaches can get uncomfortable with the feeling that the players have a portion of decision-making ability as partners within the team. Because the coach's position is on the line and because the coach has more experience making decisions of this type, the coach dictates most of the policies and procedures surrounding team members as individuals and as a group.

On the other hand, players may feel uncomfortable with shared ownership because they may not be willing to do the things necessary for the team to win, not because they lack the ability, but because they lack confidence in themselves and in the coach. The players find safety in allowing the coaches to make all the decisions for the team—that way, the players are not responsible for the outcome. What's more, they may be afraid that if they make a poor decision, the coach will become irate. If that happens, the team suffers an untimely setback.

In short, helping young athletes to realize that they are not the only members of the team and that the team isn't only about them may require some strict teaching. The bench remains a powerful teacher. If you have players on your team who aren't willing to subordinate themselves to the good of the team, then they probably won't subordinate themselves to your coaching. In that case, they represent a cancer to your team. You can treat the cancer with bench time, or you may have to remove the cancer altogether. Still, when the team sees you defending the value of the team before any one individual or even your reputation, they will rally around you and the cause of shared progress and team advancement.

The payoff of shared ownership is greater team unity and poise under adversity. The players are unified when they are indeed co-owners and co-contributors. When team members hold similar goals, have a great desire to execute a plan to achieve those goals, and a willingness to be held accountable to the plan, the team is united in its mindset and purpose. Because the purpose of the team is secure, the team is not easily distracted under pressure. Therefore, trust and confidence are high, as is the sense of satisfaction in the relationships among team members. In many ways, the term "family" applies because the relationships become mutual investments in the well-being of others—an inspiring partnership in the unabashed pursuit of excellence.

"TIP-INS" FOR...Building Shared Ownership
1. Be willing to let go of ego to attract more potent influence.
2. Model trust by giving people the freedom to fail along with the freedom to succeed.
3. Foster solid channels of communication which allow the coach to evaluate rather than dictate the course of team activities.
4. Find ways to make the last person on the team feel valuable, and you will be able to create a unified team culture.
5. Teach the team leaders to assume some of the responsibility for making sure the rest of the team or individuals are "on the same sheet of music." Build both leaders and followers.

25

Best Player, Best Worker

Each one should test his own actions. Then he can take pride in himself, without comparing himself to somebody else (Gal. 6:4).

Most of us who appreciate athletic competition enjoy the feeling of demonstrating superiority over someone, and of comparing our abilities to theirs only to find that we are better than them. But one of the surest ways to impede your own progress is to take the focus away from your own improvement and growth and begin comparing yours to someone else.

For young and immature players, a sure way of determining who's cool and who's not is by the physical prowess they possess. Ever notice that the most popular players on a little kids' baseball team are the most talented players? Status is easily achieved if you can run fast, hit the ball far, jump high, or perform grand feats of strength. But all of this is set up on the basis of a comparison to other people or some external standard. Kids fail to grasp the importance of maximizing their already gifted physiques by applying the polish of hard work, self-discipline, and focus, persevering past both the successes and failures to the point of truly understanding what their best really is. Your best player can be your greatest ally or your worst nightmare.

To create the best team possible, we, as coaches, must work extremely hard at doing everything possible to ensure that our best player is also our hardest worker. If our most talented player sets a high standard for work each day in practice, then our team is likely to move in a similar fashion.

Conversely, if the best player goes 50% in practice, then there is absolutely no way you can have as good a team as possible. Other players will consciously or unconsciously resent either that player or you, as the coach, for either allowing that player to get by doing less or expecting other players to do more.

Generally, more one-on-one exchanges are needed with this "best player." As the coach, we must emphasize the significance of the player's impact on teammates. We can share with the player the effects of his/her work ethic on the others and instruct about the importance of an individual work ethic with long-term team results, both personally and for the team. When the best player understands these principles and begins to put them into practice, then we have taken a big step in establishing the standard for work that is necessary for our entire team. When the best player is slow to buy in to these principles, additional meetings should be held to invest whatever time is appropriate to accomplish this desired goal of the coaching staff. The bench may be a great teacher as well, communicating far more effectively than your words because, after all, what performer wants to be on the bench while the game is in progress? Your actions in addressing this particular coaching challenge will send a powerful message to the rest of the team, because they, too, are often measuring themselves to this player. As the team matures and your instruction in this matter takes hold, the best player will become a great servant by providing a strong example to the team. In addition, the team will recognize how valuable the contribution from the best player really is.

Communication, in this instance is a huge priority, and the standard that we hold for our best player must not be compromised. If we invest time with our best player, generally we can accomplish the desired result. We must be careful to not mistake our best player's effectiveness in practice for the highest level of effort. Many times the most talented players can be effective at 70% effort. This is especially true for high school and middle school levels where one player may simply be much more talented than all of his/her teammates. In college, the luxury usually exists in having other good players that are likely to challenge the best player's level of interest.

"TIP-INS" FOR...Leading the Best Player, Best Worker
1. Communicate clearly and consistently about work ethic.
2. Never mistake activity for achievement regarding the best player.
3. Set standards higher for the best player because they have more to give and have been blessed with more.
4. Challenge the best player to compete against self rather than against a comparison to someone else.
5. Just as Jesus spent more time with his disciples, so too must you and I in coaching our best players—they simply have different and greater responsibilities than others.

26

Chemistry: A Key Ingredient
of Great Teams

*Do everything without complaining or arguing, so that
you may become blameless and pure, children of God
without fault in a crooked and depraved generation,
in which you shine like stars in the universe* (Phil.
2:14-15).

The Apostle Paul understood the importance of not only
working together as a team, but also harmonizing individuals into something greater than a collection of parts. In so
doing, Paul recognized that humility and subordination are
the catalysts to reaching new heights. Indeed, Paul referred
to those people who could come together in this way as
stars—bright points of light against a backdrop of blackness.
Many coaches have said that great teams are made up of
great players. This is, in part, true but over simplified. Great
teams have many more things going for them than just
gifted players. There is a relational dynamic that brings more
strength to the group than merely the aggregate talents.

One aspect of great teams is the notion of chemistry.

While chemistry, on many teams, seems elusive, coaches can use specific approaches to foster a collective attitude and collective effort.

Chemistry is beyond just playing well together. Chemistry is a bond of love and respect built on a trusting relationship. Chemistry is far more than liking or disliking someone. Pettiness of this sort among team members only creates splits and divisions. On the other hand, the kind of love mentioned above reflects a tough-minded optimism about the other person's abilities to contribute all the effort they have. Love is not a choice for the faint of heart. Love requires guts.

For example, if we are teammates, I may not like what you do or what you say, but because we are bound by a common purpose and common goal, I must sacrifice my personal likes and dislikes for our mutual benefit. If the entire team can adopt this unconditional attitude, the team chemistry will ignite and there will be a unified mindset and purposeful spirit, the weapons of great warriors.

"TIP-INS" FOR...Creating Chemistry
1. Lead by example; be trustworthy by keeping your promises to your athletes.
2. Practice the art of relating; if X's and O's are the science of coaching, then relationships are the art. Building and blending solid relationships takes time and consistent, purposeful practice.
3. Remember: we never control what we get in sport or life, only what we give. Focus on your contribution rather than what someone else may not be giving.
4. The spiritual currency of chemistry is shared

commitment to a singular goal. Team effectiveness requires physical talent, but truly committed goal-seekers establish a common currency that multiplies effort.

5. There is a big difference between friendship and respect on a team. Respect does not require people to be friends, but rather to appreciate differences. Embracing differences makes teams stronger.

27

More Than Teamwork

All the believers were together and had everything in common. Selling their possessions and goods, they gave to anyone as he had need. Everyday they continued to meet together in the temple courts. They broke bread in their homes and ate together with glad and sincere hearts, praising God and enjoying the favor of all the people. And the Lord added to their number daily those who were being saved (Acts 2: 44-47).

What a wonderful picture we have of a group cooperating in a common endeavor in the verses above. So many of the necessary ingredients in authentically cohesive teams are there, giving us a model of how it is supposed to be for our families, teams, and churches.

Their selflessness is shown by holding everything in common; there were no selfish agendas, no self-aggrandizement, and no ego. They held common values and beliefs—particularly the value of service—because they gave to others as they had need. They each gave consistent effort and received consistent discipline, choosing to meet together at the temple to stay sharp in the faith, sharing the fundamentals of their faith as they spoke of Jesus and salvation. They all had a common desire for camaraderie and enjoyed each other's company so much that they wanted to eat together. They all displayed a sincerity of character. And as they praised God, living out the ideal of the collective faith in Jesus, they found favor with people, and the Lord added to their number. He blessed their work, and people were being saved. Does this kind of collective focus and endeavor sound like your team?

While doing some research into the question of what makes athletic coaches and teams great, I discovered some material on Coach Krzyzewski and the Duke Blue Devils. One concept that grabbed my attention as I was paging through the introduction of *A Season is A Lifetime* (a book by Bill Brill and Coach K), was something Coach K referred to as collective responsibility. In Coach K's straightforward style, he succinctly described something akin to teamwork, but it was distinctly different as his description illustrated something deeper. As I read more about the concept and began to understand it, it occurred to me that this was something deeper than merely working together toward team goals.

As Coach K explained,

We are all accountable for the actions of our group. If something goes wrong or if we lose a game, we do not blame anyone. We take responsibility for it and try to ensure it *does not* happen again. When something goes right or when we win a game, we all take responsibility for it and try to ensure it *does* happen again.

136

During the course of a practice or game, each of our players will contribute in different ways and at different times. They cannot possibly be expected to contribute the same way all the time. However, while each will contribute differently, each has an equal responsibility to contribute everything he has every time we play or practice.

What struck me as different were the words "accountable" and "responsibility." When they explain the concept of teamwork, many coaches use analogies of passing the ball to a teammate, setting a screen to free up a shooter, or rotating defensively to help. Yet, in this concept, collective responsibility means more than just passing and screening and defensive rotation to help teammates. Collective responsibility puts teeth in the notion that we are: 1) accountable for our contribution to the group and 2) have a responsibility to make a maximum contribution when called upon to do so. Accountability and responsibility are daring concepts for many people, but they are essential ingredients needed to maximize group performance.

It seems to me that this concept speaks volumes for individual players and coaches. As we look at our personal involvement in the games we love and coach, each of us is accountable for our contribution to the game's betterment as well as responsible for our conduct toward producing that betterment. To the extent we accept being accountable and responsible, we become leaders, regardless of rank or title.

As a leadership concept, collective responsibility implies that, as a group, we are connected by shared values and purpose, bonded by a set of common goals, linked by common desires, and dedicated to a common mission. We are connected by a common enthusiasm for a sport and in our desire to pursue excellence in its activities. Our common goals involve the theme of excellence as individuals and as it pertains to our athletic programs. Our common desires are likely centered around personal success through service to the Lord Jesus, our families, teams, colleagues, and communities, manifested in outstanding coaching and leadership. And our common mission involves the noble task of making a positive difference in the lives of young people, to the glory of God.

The strength of collective responsibility eludes many because of resistance to being accountable and responsible. The fear of being found out as incompetent or lacking in knowledge about a sport or about coaching in general is very scary to many young or inexperienced coaches. These two attributes represent the "little things that lead to big things." Many people deem these principles to be unpopular and in many cases unnecessary, because they expose their weaknesses.

Most coaches know, however, that champions are usually those individuals who are not afraid to examine their weaknesses because they reveal places where they must increase their strength in order to improve. And the great ones in sports have always been those who do things which others may not understand or like or simply choose not to do.

In developing personal accountability, individuals openly enlist the support of trusted peers in staying on track in both attitude and action. In accepting responsibility for one's actions, individuals gain a sense of confidence and control, knowing they have claimed ownership of their efforts. By shirking personal responsibility, coaches usually compromise their own performance by essentially empowering someone or something else and defeating themselves. Collective responsibility becomes difficult at best.

Naturally, we don't want to enlist accountability partners whose hearts aren't right and who are not in a position, either personally or professionally, to help us progress. In short, we need to find mentors, people who check up on us and hold our feet to the fire in terms of staying focused on the mission, and those who will assist us to mature and grow as coaches. When coaches humbly seek the counsel and wisdom of a mentor it keeps us "coachable," because as soon as we think we have it all figured out, we're vulnerable and impotent as servants; our hearts and minds are deceived, and we are no longer in a position of leadership. Our humility as coaches is vital, because before we can serve others, we must first kneel at their feet, pick up the towel, rather than the coach's clipboard or whistle, and follow Jesus' example.

As leaders, let us not lose hope that our efforts and contributions can and do make a positive difference in the lives of other people. As a coach, why not adopt an orientation toward collective responsibility?

"TIP-INS" FOR...Building Teamwork
1. A compelling mission for the team gives credibility to the notion of being accountable and responsible to the team.
2. Working together can be done without emotion or passion or relationships, but you'll end up with a mediocre result. The dynamics of the team that give it

life are human dynamics—channel the collective energy by teaching and facilitating good relationships.

3. Find a wise mentor or role model and listen twice as much as you speak.

4. Accepting responsibility is a wonderful example for young athletes to witness in the coach—no excuses, no blame, just honesty and forthright progress.

5. Being accountable and responsible doesn't necessarily mean that the door is open to severe and harsh scrutiny and negative criticism, unless it's earned. Instead, the intent is for wholly constructive and positive feedback, directed at growth and development.

28

The Forgotten Players

Now as the church submits to Christ, so also wives should submit to their husbands in everything. Husbands, love your wives, just as Christ loved the church and gave himself up for her (Eph. 5:24-25).

I bet the last time you looked down your bench, you overlooked some key players on your team. Their contributions are absolutely essential, yet they are seldom called into the forefront for others to recognize. It is quite possible these team members don't complain or pout when you don't acknowledge their presence. Each of them is usually content to be a role player, not wanting attention, but is ready to step in when you give the signal. Until then, each player maintains the role of being in the shadows, trusting that you haven't forgotten them, allowing you unencumbered progress to pursue the activities and interests of your team, always making contributions and sacrifices for the good of the team. Each of them is a living testimony to unselfishness, decency, loyalty, and commitment—virtues many believe make for a winner.

Who are they? Whether we, as coaches, recognize it or not, our spouses and families establish the underlying foundation of our coaching success that cannot be forgotten.

In a growing number of cases, unfortunately, coaches have forgotten. Some of us have failed to see the bigger picture of their contributions and we took their efforts for granted. They agreed to accept us unconditionally, for better or worse, but we, in retrospect, were deceived, misreading the situation by placing a far greater emphasis on success on the field rather than success at home. Eventually, we came to the point where relationships at home could not bear the pressure, and the "team" came apart.

We exhausted ourselves in practice for what we thought was the good of the sports program, only to come home and realize that there was no energy left to give to those we truly cared about the most. Rather than gaining perspective, we pushed harder, for longer hours, watching more tape—relentlessly—only to realize that the potential for a loving and safe "home court advantage" was slowly eroding away. A good team self-destructed, not because of one person's faults in particular, but because of poor choices which lead to even worse misunderstandings.

Others of us have found peace, if not contentment and tranquility, on the "home" team because our spouses have made it so easy. They manage the "home court" so well that we are liberated to take care of the team outside. This kind of "home" team is great because we coaches can focus our energies and attentions more keenly on helping athletes perform better. At the same time, however, there is the danger of getting too comfortable, too relaxed in this arrangement, taking for granted the relationships at home. Each relationship at home needs the coach's personalized attention even more than relationships outside. The "team" never says anything because they love us and are happy when they see us happy, but they have needs, too.

Still others of us have found the coach/spouse relationship to be one great adventure, never exactly knowing what will be around the next turn, but holding onto each other for dear life anyway, consciously and continually supporting each other. This type of home team is strong and full of life because the Spirit of Jesus fills the marriage and keeps the flames of faith, hope, and love ablaze. The hard work of always being emotionally prepared for an "up" or a "down" is overshadowed by the sense of adventure, the bond of trust and love, and realizing that it is the journey of life itself that draws the ties of marriage and family more tightly together. The focus is on the process, the adventure of maturing as a couple and family, rather than on the outcomes. Even so, the adventure of the coaching life is not always one fun ride after another...

Because the spouse loves the coach, the spouse may not say anything about feeling lonely or distant, because they don't want to distract us from our coaching. Indeed, the spouse sacrifices personal needs for the good of the coach's team. Not wanting to disrupt or complain, the spouse lets the coach pursue his/her coaching dreams. This loving gift is the kind of sacrifice that deserves the coach's unconditional respect, gratitude, and love. What, then, does the coach give in return?

As coaches, we ask our athletes to set aside personal agendas for the team welfare and the concept can be taught through our models. Sacrifice, after all, is a manifestation of love and respect for someone else. Just as a screen is a type of sacrifice necessary to make an offense work, so is not bringing home recruit folders or practice films in order for the coach to focus on spending meaningful, non-preoccupied time at home.

Nurturing a loving marriage relationship—a loving "home team"— while building a stable home environment of unconditional trust and mutual respect is perhaps one of the greatest challenges a coach can face. For sure, the storms that most coaches encounter on the open water of a turbulent season are enough for us to want out of the boat. And, like Peter, we will surely drown unless we fix our eyes on Jesus and reach out to Him to rescue us and save us from ourselves.

In the end, the defining moments of a season, and more importantly, of a marriage, those of which cameras never see or fans or friends never know, are really about relationships forged through adversity, built on love, and reinforced by selfless sacrifice. Solid relationships built from bonds of trust, love, caring, and respect provide a reserve from which to draw strength, particularly when interpersonal communications get fragmented, quality time is virtually non-existent, and late-night microwave meals alone become the standard diet. The lifestyle of a coach and his/her family is indeed unique and loaded with challenges. Can these challenges be met with a partial team effort? When was the last time you looked down your bench and really saw what was there?

"TIP-INS" FOR...The Forgotten Players
1. Use travel time to and from practice to reset and refocus your priorities. When you get home from practice, your

morning, just beyond the first sand dune, you will arrive at a field of colored rocks as far as the eye can see. In this field, you will find red, yellow, green, and white rocks. If you are willing to collect as many colored rocks as you can and carry them with you to the end of your journey, upon your arrival at your destination you will be both very glad and very sad."

The three men began to look at one another, confused and skeptical, not quite sure what they had just witnessed. As they looked back across the stream, the figure vanished as mysteriously as it had appeared. They shrugged at his disappearance and retired for the evening.

An hour or so into the first day of their journey, suddenly, just as the figure had described, they came over the first sand dune to find the ground covered with colored rocks. They immediately walked into the field and began picking them up and placing them in their leather traveling bags. Curiously, they looked at each other, none of them exactly sure why they were picking up the rocks other than that it was what the figure had said to do. So, once they had gathered all they could carry, they continued on their way.

When the rock field was several hours behind them, it began to get very hot. Even though it was just their first day of travel, they were now carrying extra weight, making each man's legs and back very tired. The struggle gradually began to wear them down.

"Stop!" one of the men shouted. "This is the most ridiculous thing I've ever done—carrying rocks across the desert because some apparition told me to! Both of you surely realize we're only prolonging our trip out here in the heat and sand by doing so. We're slowing ourselves down! Why don't you dump out your rocks just as I am? We'll travel much faster—and besides, I don't believe the figure in the mist was real at all. At this point, I am far more concerned about making progress than I am about acquiring a collection of colored rocks. The quicker we get to the other side of the desert, the quicker we can relax and enjoy ourselves."

Well, his two colleagues weren't quite as willing to dump out their rocks at that moment. They looked at each other, waiting for the other to say or do something. When it was apparent that neither of them was going to follow what the first man said, they were back on their way and soon made camp as the sun was beginning to set.

As the three companions began their second day of traveling, it soon felt almost hotter than the day before. The sultry winds swirled around them kicking up sand and dust. It wasn't long before one of the men who had kept his rocks called a halt to their procession. The seed of doubt planted yesterday had taken root.

"You know," he said, "if I would have been smart, I would have dumped my rocks out yesterday, too! My legs and my back are very sore, my throat is parched, and my feet feel blistered inside my shoes. What's more, I slept terribly last night, and the last thing I want to be doing is carrying around extra weight. I'm dumping these stupid things out right now!"

As the last rock tumbled out of his bag and hit the sand with a thud, the two who had rid themselves of their rocks turned to see what the third man would do. As you might imagine, the solitary man left standing with his rocks felt the penetrating stares of his friends, as if they were asking, "Well, what are you waiting for?"

"Friends," he said, "I will not hold it against you, should

you decide to go on ahead. As you both have said, carrying these rocks seems to make no sense at all. However, I am willing to continue to carry my rocks with me if only to satisfy my curiosity. I am not certain what the figure meant by "both very sad and very glad," but I have done unusual things before and I will surely do them in the future. If there is exceeding gladness or sadness in the end for me—fine. It is quite possible that nothing at all will happen as I reach the other side. As for me, I can get to the other side on my own if the two of you feel the desire to go more quickly."

"Very well," they said. "The three of us will remain together through this evening. In the morning the two of us will travel ahead and wait for you in town."

The third and final day of the journey found the three traveling companions separated—two traveling with the conversation of a friend, one traveling with the conversation of his own thoughts. Naturally, the two men who had dumped their rocks arrived in town much earlier than did their colleague. They had kept their minds occupied as they talked to one another, and they had soon crossed the remaining miles of sand.

As for the third man, he had been left to his own persistence, determination, and resolve. He was not about to bail out as his traveling companions had done. He was not going to quit even though the outcome was uncertain. Somehow, he still had faith in what the apparition had told him.

Once arriving in town, the two men quickly found some shade from the sun and some cool drinks and began to unwind from their tiring and unusual trip. About that time, as they looked back out over the sandy dunes through which they had just trudged, a small speck appeared on the horizon which captured their attention. As the two men studied it, they realized it was their friend slowly making his way toward them.

After some time had gone by, the third man stumbled toward them, near exhaustion, still clutching the bags of rocks he had collected. Helping their exhausted and nearly dehydrated friend to a shaded resting place and finding him a cold drink, the two who had dumped their rocks started to become very curious as they recalled what the mysterious figure had said. So, after a few moments, they asked the third man to look in his traveling bags to see what if anything had happened to the rocks.

Slowly and cautiously, the third man pulled open the draw strings of his bags, carefully revealing the contents of each bag. To all of their amazement, the bags were loaded with jewels! The red rocks had turned to rubies, the green rocks had turned to emeralds, the yellow rocks had turned to gold, and the white rocks had turned to diamonds.

As the third man collected himself, blinking and wide-eyed in disbelief, the words of the misty figure whispered in his mind, "You'll be both very sad and very glad...." Strangely, even as those words gently faded from his mind, he began to feel both joy and sorrow building in his heart. At that moment, the meaning of his struggle across the desert became vividly clear. What had seemed meaningless in the middle of the desert had taken on new significance. He was unable to either laugh or cry—he was indeed "both very glad and very sad." Because of his tremendous new-found wealth, he was naturally overjoyed! His days as a common laborer were over, forever!

Yet, when he thought about all the colored rocks that had laid before him in the desert, and all the further opportunity and possibility that could have been, for him as well as his friends, he was deeply saddened. Indeed, his friends had been short-sighted, selfish, and impatient.

His friends, too, were filled with emotion because they also had the same opportunity before them, but instead chose to take the easy way. They felt resentment toward their persistent friend. They were envious, frustrated, disappointed, and remorseful. How could their attitudes have been so impatient and their will so undisciplined? If they had only had the maturity and wisdom and resolve to persevere in the face of great difficulty, they too would have found themselves both very sad and very glad, content in their choice to pay the price, delaying gratification for a promised reward. The fulfilled promise of riches in the future would surely have been worth the struggle in the present.

Have you heard from the Spirit recently? Found any brightly colored rocks along your path?

About the Author

DAN GERDES is no stranger to collegiate athletics and coaching, having both played and coached college basketball at the NCAA Division III level. In addition, he has invested a good deal of his education studying the nature and effects of great coaching and leadership, crossing paths with many of America's most well-known college athletic coaches, military commanders, and various elected government officials. He is a sought after speaker and consultant on topics pertaining to leadership, coaching, and mental excellence, earning his doctorate in applied Sport Psychology from the University of Kansas.

Dan is President and founder of Renewing the Heart, LLC, an organization committed to proclaiming the hope and life-giving potential found in Jesus Christ. He is currently a member of the Health and Human Performance faculty at Central Missouri State University in Warrensburg, Missouri. He and his wife, Karen, have three boys, one at home with Jesus, and two at home with them.

To contact the author
for speaking engagements, please write:

Daniel A. Gerdes, Ph.D.
c/o Renewing the Heart, LLC
P.O. Box 217
Warrensburg, MO 64093
email: dkgerdes@earthlink.net